BARBER SHOP CHRONICLES

Inua Ellams

BARBER SHOP CHRONICLES

OBERON BOOKS
LONDON

WWW.OBERONBOOKS.COM

First published in 2017 by Oberon Books Ltd
521 Caledonian Road, London N7 9RH
Tel: +44 (0) 20 7607 3637 / Fax: +44 (0) 20 7607 3629
e-mail: info@oberonbooks.com
www.oberonbooks.com

A catalogue record for this book is available from the British
Library.

PB ISBN: 9781786821782
E ISBN: 9781786821799

Cover: Photograph by Dean Chalkley
         Designed by National Theatre Graphic Design Studio

Printed and bound by Marston Book Services, Didcot, UK.
eBook conversion by CPI Group (UK) Ltd, Croydon, CR0 4YY.

SAMUEL	**Fisayo Akinade**
WALLACE / TIMOTHY / MOHAMMED / TINASHE	**Hammed Animashaun**
KWABENA / BRIAN / FABRICE / OLAWALE	**Peter Bankolé**
MUSA / ANDILE / MENSAH	**Maynard Eziashi**
TANAKA / FIIFI	**Simon Manyonda**
TOKUNBO / PAUL / SIMPHIWE	**Patrice Naiambana**
EMMANUEL	**Cyril Nri**
ETHAN	**Kwami Odoom**
ELNATHAN / BENJAMIN / DWAIN	**Sule Rimi**
KWAME / SIMON / WOLE	**Abdul Salis**
ABRAM / OHENE / SIZWE	**David Webber**
WINSTON / SHONI	**Anthony Welsh**

Director	**Bijan Sheibani**
Designer	**Rae Smith**
Lighting Designer	**Jack Knowles**
Movement Director	**Aline David**
Sound Designer	**Gareth Fry**
Music Director	**Michael Henry**
Fight Director	**Kev McCurdy**
Barber Consultant	**Peter Atakpo**
Company Voice Work	**Charmian Hoare**
Dialect Coach	**Hazel Holder**
Staff Director	**Stella Odunlami**
Dramaturgs	**Sebastian Born**
	Tom Lyons

WORLD PREMIERE
Dorfman Theatre, London 7 June 2017
At West Yorkshire Playhouse from 12 to 29 July 2017

SETTING
Barber shops in Peckham, London; Johannesburg, South Africa; Harare, Zimbabwe; Kampala, Uganda; Lagos, Nigeria; and Accra, Ghana.

Barber Shop Chronicles was co-commissioned by Fuel and the National Theatre. Development funded by Arts Council England with the support of Fuel, National Theatre Studio, West Yorkshire Playhouse, The Binks Trust, British Council ZA, Òran Mór and A Play, a Pie and a Pint.

National Theatre

The National Theatre makes world-class theatre that is entertaining, challenging and inspiring. And we make it for everyone.

We stage up to 30 productions at our South Bank home each year, ranging from reimagined classics – such as Greek tragedy and Shakespeare – to modern masterpieces and new work by contemporary writers and theatre-makers. The work we make strives to be as open, as diverse, as collaborative and as national as possible. Much of that new work is researched and developed at the New Work Department: we are committed to nurturing innovative work from new writers, directors, creative artists and performers. Equally, we are committed to education, with a wide-ranging Learning programme for all ages in our Clore Learning Centre and in schools and communities across the UK.

The National's work is also seen on tour throughout the UK and internationally, and in collaborations and co-productions with regional theatres. Popular shows transfer to the West End and occasionally to Broadway. Through National Theatre Live, we broadcast live performances to cinemas around the world.

National Theatre: On Demand. In Schools makes acclaimed, curriculum-linked productions free to stream on demand in every primary and secondary school in the country. Online, the NT offers a rich variety of innovative digital content on every aspect of theatre.

We do all we can to keep ticket prices affordable and to reach a wide audience, and use our public funding to maintain artistic risk-taking, accessibility and diversity.

Chair of NT Board **Sir Damon Buffini**
Deputy Chair **Kate Mosse**
Director of the National Theatre **Rufus Norris**
Executive Director **Lisa Burger**

National Theatre
Box office and information
+44 (0) 20 7452 3000
National Theatre, Upper Ground,
London SE1 9PX

nationaltheatre.org.uk

·⎺fueL

Fuel aims to catalyse positive change in the world by producing new live performance. Founded in 2004, Fuel works to develop, create and share a programme of artistic work created by outstanding artists with and for people across the UK and beyond.

Fuel Director Kate McGrath and Inua Ellams met in 2008, after Kate saw the beginnings of what became Inua's first play, *The 14th Tale*, at BAC. Fuel helped Inua develop this debut and produced it, premiering it at the Edinburgh Festival, winning a Fringe First, touring it in the UK and internationally and presenting it at the National Theatre. Since that first meeting, Fuel has worked closely with Inua, producing *Untitled, Knight Watch, The Long Song Goodbye, Black T-shirt Collection, The Spalding Suite, An Evening with an Immigrant* and *Barber Shop Chronicles* since its inception.

fueltheatre.com

@fueltheatre

Director: **Kate McGrath**
Executive Director: **Ed Errington**
Head of Production: **Stuart Heyes**
Head of Programme: **Emilie Wiseman**
Projects Producers : **Niamh Dilworth**, **Sarah Jane Murray**, **Sarah Wilson-White**
Projects Managers: **Hattie Gregory, Charlotte Hodkinson, Emily Thommes**
Administrator: **Caroline Simonsen**

Catalysts and Trustees*: **Ben Chamberlain, Sean Egan** (Chair)*, **Lilli Geissendorfer*, Joe Hallgarten*, Akiya Henry*, Caroline Jones, James Mackenzie-Blackman, Michael Morris, Rob O'Rahilly, Sarah Preece, Jenny Sealey, Tina Temple Morris, Shail Thaker*, John Tiffany,** and **Nick Williams*.**

"Fuel is an inspiration." **The Guardian**

Registered Charity No: 1149680
Registered as a company limited by guarantee in England: 7935786

WEST YORKSHIRE
PLAYHOUSE

Welcome to the home of incredible stories

There has been a Playhouse in Leeds for almost 50 years; from 1968 to 1990 as Leeds Playhouse and then with the opening of a brand new theatre on its current Quarry Hill site it became West Yorkshire Playhouse.

West Yorkshire Playhouse is a leading UK producing theatre; a cultural hub, a place where people gather to tell and share stories and to engage in world class theatre. We make work which is pioneering and relevant, seeking out the best companies and artists to create inspirational theatre in the heart of Yorkshire. From large scale spectacle, to intimate performance we develop and make work for our stages, for found spaces, for touring, for schools and community centres. Our 2015/16 production of Chitty Chitty Bang Bang played to over 500,000 people across the country – our production of Beryl played to 100 in a village hall in Wickenby, Lincolnshire. We create work to entertain and inspire.

As dedicated collaborators, we work regularly with other theatres from across the UK, independent producers, and some of the most distinctive, original voices in theatre today. We develop work with established practitioners and find, nurture and support new voices that ought to be heard. We cultivate new talent by providing creative space for new writers, emerging directors, companies and individual theatre makers to refine their practice.

Alongside our work for the stage we are dedicated to providing creative engagement opportunities that excite and stimulate. We build, run and sustain projects which reach out to everyone from refugee communities, to young people and students, to older communities and people with learning disabilities. At the Playhouse there is always a way to get involved.

West Yorkshire Playhouse – Vital theatre.

Artistic Director **James Brining**
Executive Director **Robin Hawkes**
Chairman of the Board **Sir Rodney Brooke CBE**

Leeds Theatre Trust Limited. Charity No. 255460
VAT No. 545 4890 17 Company No. 926862, England Wales
Registered address Playhouse Square, Quarry Hill, Leeds, LS2 7UP

Thanks to:

Krystle Lai, Kate McGrath, Bijan Sheibani, Stella Odunlami, Fisayo Akinade, Hammed Animashaun, Peter Bankolé, Maynard Eziashi, Simon Manyonda, Patrice Naiambana, Cyril Nri, Kwami Odoom, Sule Rimi, Abdul Salis, David Webber, Anthony Welsh, Rae Smith, Jack Knowles, Aline David, Gareth Fry, Michael Henry, Kev McCurdy, Peter Atakpo, Charmian Hoare, Hazel Holder, Sebastian Born, Tom Lyons, Rufus Norris, Ben Power, Emily McLaughlin, Nina Steiger, Wendy Spon, Douglas Ejikeme Nwokolo, Michael Ekewere, Ros Brooke-Taylor, Nick Starr, Peter Nice, Nadine Patel, Fusi Olateru, The British Council, Jo and Alison Elliot, Rambisayi Marufu, Billy Wolf, Christina Elliot, Alice Massey, Chesta Clarke, Shonisani-Lethole, Milisuthando Bongela, Mandal Mazibuko, Dwain, Abel, Jay, Thabiso Mohare, Lebo Mashile, Tendai, Jessica Horn, Michale Onsando, Daniel, Aleya Kassam, Njoki Ngumi, Maimouna Jallow, Ian Arunga, Brian Munene, George Gachara, Njeri Wagacha, Mugsas Blick, Phiona Okumu, Cathy Adengo, Beverly Namozo, Simon, Alex, Dre Jackson, Jimmy, Patricia Okelowange. Jessica Horn, Jude Atebe, Wallace Egbe, Fiona Hecksher, Wana Udobang, Tolu Ogunlesi, Wole Oguntokun, Adreonke Adebanjo, Kenneth Uphopho, Ore Disu, Tj Owusu. Mary Owusu-Bempah, Seth EboArthur, Nii Ayikwei Parkes, Fiifi Ayikwei Parkes, Omara Ayikwei Parkes, Marianne San Miguel, Billie McTernan, Belinda Boakye, Belinda Zhawi. Bridget, Anna & Joseph Minamore, Leeto Thale, Simon Godwin, Mensah Bediako, Daniel Ward, Jo Servi, Syrus Lowe, Denver Isaac, Ekow Quartey, Tunji Lucas, Tunji Kasim, Kobna Holdbrook-Smith, Seun Shote, Kurt Egyiawan, Ivanno Jeremiah, Daniel Francis, Calvin Demba, Sope Dirisu, Daniel Poyser, Poetra Asantewa, Shade & Kay Odunlami, Xavier de Sousa, Jamie Hadley and the team at The Cut Festival of Barbering, and the late David MacLennan and his team at
A Play, A Pie and A Pint at Òran Mór.

By the time a man realises
his father was right,
he already has a son
who thinks he's wrong.

— Charles Wadsworth

For:
Inua Snr, Emmanuel, Michael, Malachi & Ethan.

SCENE 1 – PROLOGUE

LAGOS // CHARACTERS:

TOKUNBO – Nigerian. Late 60s.

WALLACE – Nigerian. Early 20s.

// 06:00 A tiny shack of a barbershop. MR TOKUNBO, sleeping on a thin mattress on the floor, is woken by a banging on the door.

TOKUNBO: Eh! What time is it?

> *// Banging.*

> Chineke!

> *// Banging.*

> We're not open.

> *// Banging.*

TOKUNBO: I said we're not open!

WALLACE: Please!

TOKUNBO: Come back at 8 o'clock.

WALLACE: No. That's two hours from now!

TOKUNBO: That's when we open.

WALLACE: Please!

TOKUNBO: Please what?! We are not open.

WALLACE: Help me! Na emergency.

> *(Beat.)*

> Abeg jor!

> *(Beat.)*

> Oga, please! I would not come if/ it wasn't important. Please, I'm begging you.

TOKUNBO: Okay, I'm coming! I dey come!

// TOKUNBO opens the door.

TOKUNBO: What's the matter?

WALLACE: I need a hair cut.

TOKUNBO: In the whole of Lagos, whole of Nigeria am I the only one?

WALLACE: You were close by.

TOKUNBO: I'm sleeping!

WALLACE: Na emergency.

TOKUNBO: It is 6 a.m!

WALLACE: Job interview is at 9 o'clock and e go take three hours reach.

TOKUNBO: I need to sleep!

WALLACE: I need this job. Please sir.

(Beat.)

TOKUNBO: Oya, come in.

WALLACE: God go bless you. Thank you so much.

// TOKUNBO goes to start a generator.

WALLACE: Wait, I will turn it on. Thank you sir.

// TOKUNBO gathers the equipment in silence.

TOKUNBO: Come and sit down.

WALLACE: My name is Wallace.

(Beat.)

TOKUNBO: Tokunbo.

WALLACE: Mr Tokunbo, your shop, did you name it?

TOKUNBO: It's a nickname.

WALLACE: Kowope. It means/ it means.

TOKUNBO: 'Let the money be complete.'

WALLACE: *(Laughs.)* It's a good name. It's a philosophy.

TOKUNBO: *(Laughs.)* Na so now.

WALLACE: Yoruba na language sha! One small word means whole sentence for English.

TOKUNBO: Just because of the name some people say… *You barb your hair at Kowope?! Ah! Where is Kowope?* They wants to know the place through the name.

WALLACE: It's a good name, well done.

TOKUNBO: So, what d'you want?

WALLACE: Skin cut, gorimapa!

TOKUNBO: Oh? You have nice hair. I can fade it.

WALLACE: I want to look sharp, aerodynamic for interview.

TOKUNBO: What's the job?

WALLACE: Driver.

TOKUNBO: *(Laughs.)*

WALLACE: What?

TOKUNBO: The car no get roof?

WALLACE: E get now.

TOKUNBO: How skin cut go help aerodynamics?

WALLACE: Last month, my uncle Elnathan wey dey for England send me one poster for BMW Z4. Nought to 60 in 4.4 seconds! Aerodynamic! Sleek, sharp, nothing, no excess. The car is parked, but the slogan says *Zero miles per hour, never looked so fast.* I want to look like a fast driver.

TOKUNBO: *(Laughs.)* Na your money now. Why you wan drive anyway? You're intelligent man.

WALLACE: I'm driving already, I just wan work for agency. I be secondary school teacher before. I get one friend wey dey drive, e dey change car like e dey change girlfriend.

TOKUNBO: *(Laughs.)*

WALLACE: And he say his boss doesn't treat him well! He dey make forty thousand a month and he was complaining! Me na twenty I am making and I can drive... so, I come Lagos, come live with my aunty.

TOKUNBO: Eh/

WALLACE: She get car but cannot drive. One week pass, two weeks, de car dey gather dust. So, I persuade her to give me keys. She no believe say I can drive but I open gate, enter car, put am for reverse, drive out: no scratch, no crash, nothing! My aunty come talk say *Ah! Wallace! You sabi drive true true oh!*

TOKUNBO: *(Laughs.)*

WALLACE: Two weeks after, I'm driving her and her friends; they gimme small money. No be taxi be dat?

TOKUNBO: Na taxi now.

WALLACE: That's how I start.

(Beat.)

Kowope! The name sweet me sha! *Kowope.* You made it up?

TOKUNBO: No. Long time ago, long before I become director of here, one Yoruba boy I dey train, he love money too much!

WALLACE: *(Laughs.)*

TOKUNBO: At the end of the day, he will be shouting *Money! Kowope! Kowope!* And I never forget it. So when I open my shop, I come use am. That boy go be big man now, dey live for London.

WALLACE: Na so? ah. You still dey train boys?

TOKUNBO: Yes oh! In fact most times I no dey here. I dey travel go cut client for house; my clients scatter for Lagos: Ikeja, Jibowu, Mushin. That's how I started in the village,

4

up and down hills and mountains on bicycles. That was forty years ago! Then I come Lagos.

WALLACE: Forty years! Business go done change for that time now?

TOKUNBO: No be small oh! You can say is more competition now…across the whole world, barbing is changing. You just try to puts together your own package…let people know you're more better.

(Beat.)

// *TOKUNBO shows WALLACE his cut in the mirror.*

WALLACE: Ehen.

Ehen.

TOKUNBO: E done finish.

WALLACE: That was fast!

TOKUNBO: Zero miles per hour now.

WALLACE: *(Laughs.)* How much?

TOKUNBO: 1000.

WALLACE: 1000?

TOKUNBO: Na standard price.

(Beat.)

WALLACE: The ting be say…

TOKUNBO: Wetin?

WALLACE: Be like…say… Oga…

(Beat.)

TOKUNBO: Wetin?

WALLACE: I dey… I go… I no fit…

// *WALLACE runs for the door.*

TOKUNBO: Olé! Olé! Thief oh! Thief, catch am!

// *Neighbours switch on their lights.*

SCENE 2

LONDON // CHARACTERS:

SAMUEL – British & Nigerian & Pidgin. Early 20s.

EMMANUEL – Nigerian. Early 40s.

WINSTON – Caribbean. Early 30s.

KWAME – Ghanaian. Mid to late 20s.

KWABENA – Ghanaian. Early 30s.

ELNATHAN – Nigerian. Early 40s.

// 09:00 Lights come up on a barber shop. SAMUEL enters humming, switches on the television and sound system. Me Against The World by 2Pac plays. SAMUEL reduces the volume, dances around wiping surfaces, sweeping the floor.

SAMUEL: We're not open.

// Banging.

SAMUEL: I said we're not open.

// Banging.

SAMUEL: Come back in fifteen minutes.

// Banging. SAMUEL stands to open it.

SAMUEL: We are not open/ don't you understand English

ELNATHAN: Oooh! It's you! You are working here now?... I didn't think...

(Beat.)

Wow! You've grown.

(Beat.)

SAMUEL: You have to go.

ELNATHAN: I... I came to see Emmanuel.

SAMUEL: He's not here.

   (Beat.)

ELNATHAN: When is he in?

SAMUEL: I don't know.

ELNATHAN: Can you tell him I came?

   (Beat.)

   Samuel?

SAMUEL: Mmhm.

   (Beat.)

ELNATHAN: Okay. Even your haircut is the same!

   (Beat.)

   Okay, I'll be back later.

   // ELNATHAN leaves. SAMUEL paces, angrily. EMMANUEL enters from the back.

EMMANUEL: Who was that?

SAMUEL: Nobody.

EMMANUEL: Nobody?

SAMUEL: Nobody… Why? Who're you expecting?

EMMANUEL: No one.

SAMUEL: There you go.

EMMANUEL: Nobody?

SAMUEL: Nobody.

EMMANUEL: …Nobody?

SAMEUL: Nobod… is there an echo here?

EMMANUEL: Okay. What's wrong with you today?

   // EMMANUEL leaves to the back room, WINSTON arrives.

WINSTON: Who was that?

7

SAMUEL: Nobody.

WINSTON: Didn't look like nobody.

// SAMUEL and WINSTON run to collect and play fight with brooms.

WINSTON: Wha gwarn my yout'?

SAMUEL: *(Laughs.)* I'm not your youth.

WINSTON: *(Laughs.)* Ya good though yeah?

SAMUEL: Yeah. You?

WINSTON: Last night. Melissa giving me problems.

SAMUEL: She's said No to you like… six times now?

WINSTON: Ya na understand women. I'm wearing her down lickle by lickle.

SAMUEL: Women don't wear down, they toughen up, even I know that.

WINSTON: Whichever way ya put it, she cyan't resist me for ever.

SAMUEL: *(Laughs.)* Cup final today! Couldn't sleep last night! We're gonna destroy Barcelona! Wipe 'em off the pitch.

WINSTON: Chief Emmanuel will be heart-broken. Me feel fa im. Is he in yet?

SAMUEL: Yeah. *(Gestures towards the back room.)*

WINSTON: Need to resolve dis ting ya na?

SAMUEL: Need to resolve your ting with Melissa first.

WINSTON: *(Laughs.)*

// KWAME and KWABENA enter.

KWABENA & KWAME: Greetings! Greetings! Greetings! brothers. Are you open?

SAMUEL: Yes! Greetings!

EMMANUEL: Greetings.

8

SAMUEL: How body? Wetin dey?

KWABENA: God is good.

SAMUEL: Mr Religious eh?

// EMMANUEL enters.

KWABENA: Of course yes, have to be religious in these times!

ALL: *(Laugh.)*

KWABENA: This is my good friend Kwame, businessman,
just moved to London. He wanted a haircut, so I thought
where else but Three Kings?!

EMMANUEL: *(Laughs.)* I'm Emmanuel, Samuel over there,
Winston.

SAMUEL: What kind of business?

KWAME: Imports and exports to Accra, Kampala, Harare,
Johannesburg and Lagos… where my business partner is
based.

SAMUEL: The final today: Chelsea or Barcelona?

KWAME: Chelsea!

SAMUEL: Welcome to our shop. He (Emmanuel) supports
Barcelona.

ALL: Ah!

KWAME: How long has/ this shop been

// SAMUEL looks out the window, shouts out the door.

SAMUEL: Oi, get off the streets before I smack you. Me, Piss
off? Best run before I/ call your

EMMANUEL: What's happening?

SAMUEL: You didn't see?

EMMANUEL: No.

SAMUEL: They were throwing bottles at passing cars. People
watching… not saying anything.

9

KWAME: No discipline at all! And I blame the government.

SAMUEL: The government?

// KWAME sits in EMMANUEL's chair for a haircut.

KWAME: They have destroyed how you discipline children. Here, children threaten with this social services and parents can't do nothing,

SAMUEL: So you want the prime minister to slap your child?

KWABENA: *(Laughs.)* See what happened last week? With that small boy?

SAMUEL: Victor? With the afro?

KWABENA: You saw the way he talked to his mother? She said *Why didn't you text me?* He said *I'm in the chair innit?* In Ghana, the slap he would have received!

KWAME: Yes but it's not always a good thing.

EMMANUEL: When is discipline a bad thing?

KWABENA: No, it's the way… look being slapped isn't what hurts, it is the sense of justice or injustice. See, if my father lived here, the way he disciplined me, he would have gone to prison.

ALL: *(Laugh.)*

KWABENA: I would have made sure of it. Listen, one night, there was no electricity. My mother stepped on broken glass. My father got a needle to take out the shards and gave me the torchlight to hold/

EMMANUEL: Eh/

KWABENA: After ten minutes my hands started shaking; the light moving about and my father warned me, called my name three times!

ALL: Ey!

KWABENA: My hand was tired, I couldn't stop the trembling. Next time he didn't say nothing. Just one dirty slap. I couldn't hear for hours.

EMMANUEL: Ah ah! Back home, discipline is too hard. Here, too soft. Middle ground is the best.

KWABENA: There were problems I needed to talk about, but he just... One time...

(Beat.)

I really thought he would...

EMMANUEL: Sorry.

(Beat.)

SAMUEL: Is he still alive?

KWABENA: Died aged 69, God bless his soul.

KWAME: How can you say that about a man who abused you?

KWABENA: He was my father now.

ALL: Mmm.

EMMANUEL: We didn't call it abuse so it wasn't.

KWAME: That is so true. Things we don't have words for in our language don't exist. I have an autistic niece, low on the spectrum. You wouldn't tell by looking at her, but last week, my sister called crying, said she can't handle it anymore! I said *what's going on?* She said *I went to braid her hair in a Ghanaian salon* (she lives in Wales) and her daughter threw a tantrum. The place was packed, Saturday, all African clientele looking at her, shouting *Deal with your child! You are spoiling this child.* Before, I told her it's common, don't be shy, just tell people this child is autistic. She did and all hell broke loose! They were shouting *It's your fault, you are the cause of this!*

EMMANUEL: Just because she said it?

KWAME: Yeah! They told her *Slap the autism out of her!*

ALL: What?!

KWAME: *Slap it out!*

EMMANUEL: You should get involved and help.

KWAME: The aunties tell me what do I know of raising children? My hands are tied. I'm just a man.

ALL: MMM.

(Beat.)

KWAME: So, who owns this shop?

WINSTON: Chief Emmanuel.

SAMUEL: Well, my father started it.

WINSTON: Chief Emmanuel took it over.

KWAME: How long has it been open?

SAMUEL: Ten, eleven years. I just became full time three months ago.

KWAME: Your father taught you how to cut?

SAMUEL: Yeah.

KWAME: Was his father a barber too?

SAMUEL: *(Laughs.)* No, it's not like a lineage thing. My father needed someone so I stepped up.

KWAME: Okay, so no family business?

SAMUEL: *(Laughs.)* No, but that was the plan.

KWAME: Your Dad still around?

KWABENA: Kwame.

KWAME: Yes?

KWABENA: Shh.

KWAME: What?

SAMUEL: Naa, it's fine. My Dad taught me everything he knew and I ran with it.

KWAME: How old are you?

SAMUEL: I started when I was fifteen! Cutting people who only wanted gorimapa, but I was so good, so natural! Dad was loosing customers to me! Like… they go just come eh, enter shop, Dad would point to his chair, and they'd say *Naa, de short one dere.*

ALL: *(Laugh.)*

SAMUEL: Dad left, I went college, came back, did odd jobs until Emmanuel offered me a chair, I joined and *again* my reputation spread! Barbers across the whole world do different things, you just gotta put your own package together.

ALL: Mmm.

SAMUEL: This shop is alright… but my shop, my package… hmm! None of this shabby furniture, or dodgy sound system.

// WINSTON glares at SAMUEL.

KWAME: It's not that bad.

SAMUEL: It's terrible! It's gone downhill since Chief took over from my father.

WINSTON: Sam.

KWAME: What will you have different?

SAMUEL: Proper stereos! Wall to wall mirrors, fluorescent light around each chair, the best clippers, a dedicated engineer!

KWAME: So you don't see your Dad much?

SAMUEL: Not as much as I'd like to…

KWAME: What does he think?

// *EMMANUEL stops cutting and leaves to the backroom.*

KWABENA: Sorry.

SAMUEL: For what?

KWABENA: Him asking questions.

SAMUEL: Nothing wrong with asking questions.

SCENE 3

ACCRA // CHARACTERS:

ABRAM – Ghanaian. Early 30s/40s/50s.

FIIFI – Ghanaian. Early 20s.

MENSA – Ghanaian. Early 30s.

TIMOTHY – Ghanaian. Early 30s.

// 09:30. Tiny two-seater barber shop. Sofa on the left. FIIFI is getting a haircut.

FIIFI: I'm just a bit nervous.

ABRAM: Big man like you?

FIIFI: You think you are prepared for being a father and then...

(Beat.)

ABRAM: What?

FIIFI: The baby is looking up and you don't know what to say or do.

ABRAM: Do what you want!

FIIFI: I could get it wrong.

ABRAM: Is no right and wrong. Do what your father did.

FIIFI: Never! What my father did? Fathers have changed.

ABRAM: My father once said *I'm not your friend, I'm your father.* That's not changed.

FIIFI: It didn't offend you?

ABRAM: I understood him. He meant his job is to push me, not make me happy. I mean, he beat us but also we discuss politics, football, hang out...

FIIFI: Are you raising your daughter like your father raised you?

ABRAM: I play, talk, tell her I love her, but don't try to please her.

FIIFI: No beating? You are more lenient?

ABRAM: Lean-ent? Lenient?

FIIFI: You know… gentle?

ABRAM: Sometimes I just look at her, maybe she's running near water, ground is slippery, she fall down, injure herself, she learns for future. So am I *lenient* or letting her learn it herself.

FIIFI: Hmmmn

ABRAM: You? Your father? Lenient?

FIIFI: Never! Beat us mercilessly, my older brother Kwabena got the worst. One night he couldn't hold a torch steady for my father. Papa lost his temper and slapped him, cracked Kwabena's jaw and even when it healed, Kwabena never talked to him again, he left us, he left Ghana that same year. We don't know where he is.

(Beat.)

ABRAM: Your father… he spoke with his hands eh?

FIIFI: Yes, but it was the wrong kind of language.

(Beat.)

Were you around when your father died?

ABRAM: Yah.

FIIFI: You miss him?

(Beat.)

ABRAM: If you live with someone for long time, you can think what they will do or say when something happen. I don't miss him because he still here. Yesterday, my daughter did

16

good in school. Teacher said *Well done* then she said *Ma will say 'That's really good' and Pa will say 'That's okay'.*

FIIFI: *(Laughs.)*

ABRAM: She knows, just three years of age and she knows.

FIIFI: So what are you saying?

ABRAM: Listen to your child. He will show you how to raise him, he will show the right language.

// MENSA & TIMOTHY enter, engrossed in their conversation.

TIMOTHY: You know Ethiopia were never colonised? The only ones! They're as African as possible and the Ethiopian Orthodox Church predates all the colonisers'. Their king's bloodline can be traced right back to King Solomon. They have records, a thirteen month calendar, they/ are completely

MENSA: Thirteen month calendar?! That can't work! They'll be out of sync with the world.

FIIFI: But they'll be in sync with themselves! That's what matters.

MENSA: Chaleh, how are you?

ABRAM: Iye odzogbaa. Hulue teshi odzogbaa leebinee.
(I'm fine. The sun rose well this morning // Ga.)

MENSA: Leebi ye feo
(It was a beautiful morning // Ga)

TIMOTHY: What did he say?

ABRAM: I said, Meho ye, Anopayi awes pure tie
(I'm fine the sun rose well this morning // Twi)

TIMOTHY: Oh! Wo ka Twi eni Ga? You speak Ga and Twi?!

ABRAM: Of course, Good for business!

MENSAH: And you switch between sentences?

ABRAM: Easy.

MENSAH: Chaleh, that Hausaman in London...

TIMOTHY: Eh?

MENSAH: ...that spent nine years in Mexico writing a Swahili-to-Spanish dictionary...

TIMOTHY: What about him?

MENSAH: Chaleh should write us a Ga-to-Twi dictionary!

FIIFI: Nine years! Why?

TIMOTHY: So we don't have to go through English to understand each other.

ABRAM: See! See that Fiifi? Even they wants the right language eh?

FIIFI: *(Laughs.)* Yes.

MENSA: What time is the Barcelona V Chelsea Final?

FIIFI: Kick off at ten thirty.

MENSA: Chaleh, how long before you can cut my hair?

ABRAM: Nine thirty? Come back in ten minutes?

MENSA: Sure.

// MENSA and TIMOTHY stand to leave.

TIMOTHY: Supermalt?

MENSA: Guinness!

SCENE 4

LONDON // CHARACTERS:

SAMUEL – British & Nigerian & Pidgin. Early 20s.

BENJAMIN – Nigerian & Pidgin. Mid 40s.

MUSA – Nigerian & Pidgin. Mid to late 30s.

WINSTON – Caribbean. Early 30s.

// 10:00. SAMUEL is sweeping, talking to WINSTON.

WINSTON: You missed a spot.

SAMUEL: Where?

WINSTON: Dere.

SAMUEL: Where?

WINSTON: Over dere, near Emmanuel's chair.

SAMUEL: *(Kisses teeth.)* He can sweep it himself.

 (Beat.)

WINSTON: My man who come dis marning, who was dat?

SAMUEL: Who?

WINSTON: At the door?

SAMUEL: Nobody... Ahh, just trying to sell clippers.

 (Beat.)

WINSTON: Dat early? Why im ask for Emmanuel?

SAMUEL: What?

WINSTON: Im ask for Chief, directly.

SAMUEL: I don't know. Why you so bothered by this?

 (Beat.)

WINSTON: Ave to hol your tongue in front of strangers ya na.

// SAMUEL looks at WINSTON confused.

WINSTON: Just now, ya never go dat far before.

SAMUEL: I don't know what you're on about.

// BENJAMIN enters and greets WINSTON.

BENJAMIN: *(To Samuel.)* You ready for me? *(On the phone.)* Let me call you back, I'm at the barbers.

SAMUEL: Always on your phone.

BENJAMIN: Leave my phone alone; I am an international business man. I have to contactable twenty-four hours a day.

SAMUEL: Oya, come and sit down.

BENJAMIN: You want to hear a joke?

SAMUEL: Is it funny?

BENJAMIN: Na joke now.

SAMUEL: Did you invent it?

BENJAMIN: Which kind question be dat?

SAMUEL: Oya, I dey hear.

BENJAMIN: So, Hausaman, Yorubaman and Igboman are having drinks in a bar. Flies buzzing all over the place… Bzzzz plop! One fly land for Hausaman drink and he pours the whole thing away, orders fresh one. No problem. One fly land for Yorubaman drink, he pour only half the drink away where the fly land.

SAMUEL: *(Laughs.)* Eh.

BENJAMIN: Another fly bzzzz… plop! for Igboman's drink eh, he take out the fly with his fingers eh, suck the drink commot for the fly body, spit am out! *Go buy ya own!*

SAMUEL: *(Laughs.)* Go buy your own!

BENJAMIN: See how wasteful Hausaman is? Pour everything away? Yoruba, small bit. Igboman, nothing. But Hausaman?…

SAMUEL: The whole thing.

BENJAMIN: Crazy. You see, General Ojukwu saw this during the civil war! Nothing changed under President Goodluck Jonathan and nothing's changed under President Buhari, Hausa still wasteful. You know why we are still together? Simple reason o!

SAMUEL: Why?

BENJAMIN: South-South, South-West: Yoruba. South-East: Igbo. Together, we get economic power. It's why oyinbo people, the white man amalgamated Nigeria, because Hausa-North can't stand on their own; Boko Haram! Dey kill each other for their own land!

SAMUEL: We should split up?

BENJAMIN: We've split already. Only the name is why we're together.

// MUSA enters wearing a Hausa hat and goes to greet WINSTON.

BENJAMIN: Ey! Hausaman done come oh. Shhhhhhhh

SAMUEL: That's my nine thirty appointment.

BENJAMIN: It's ten o'clock!!

SAMUEL: You were late too/ so

BENJAMIN: Shhhhhh

(Beat.)

I bet he supports Barcelona.

SAMUEL: Shhh!

MUSA: Oga! Wetin dey? How is your body?

BENJAMIN: Eh?! Wetin you talk?

MUSA: I said How body?

BENJAMIN: No.

SAMUEL: Ben don't start.

BENJAMIN: Mmmm mmmm. No! You said *How IS your body?* Wetin be that one?

MUSA: Na Pidgin!

BENJAMIN: Pidgin English you mix with Proper English. People like you are killing our country.

MUSA: A ah?

BENJAMIN: E dey happen for village. I hear one small girl *My daddy will beat me, daddy will beat me.* Wetin be Daddy?

MUSA: *(Laughs.)*

BENJAMIN: *My PAPA go beat me.* No be so we dey talk? If I try that thing for home *Eh... Mummy! Mummy!* She go dey look road? *Who be mummy? Who dey come?*

WINSTON & MUSA: *(Laughs.)*

BENJAMIN: Na MAMA she know!

WINSTON: Even in Nollywood films now. *Mummy! Mummy!*

SAMUEL: *My Daddy will beat me...* e no dey sweet for mouth.

BENJAMIN: Na *Nyash* these days dem dey call *bum bum.* Wetin be *bum bum*?

MUSA: Language changes. It's the evolution of Pidgin.

BENJAMIN: Pidgin is different. It's being corrupted! When I used to play football at school, we go dey sing *We don come again oh! We don come again! Troway! Troway!* Now, my son sings *We have come again. We have come again. Throw it away. Throw it away.*

MUSA: *(Laughs.)* E don spoil oh!

BENJAMIN: You see am now?! You see it?

WINSTON: Musa is a linguist. He spent nine years in Mexico writing a Swahili-to-Spanish dictionary.

BENJAMIN: Why?

MUSA: So descendants of slaves there don't have to go through English to understand us their ancestors back home. But why you tink sey Pidgin dey die is my question. Why is pidgin dying?

BENJAMIN: Because of people like you!

MUSA: Wetin I do?

BENJAMIN: Over-educated people wey go Federal Government Colleges spoil Pidgin!

MUSA: Blame teachers! Na teachers conduct class!

BENJAMIN: No, the society tries to be so American or English. Without Pidgin we're finished!

SAMUEL: GOOD! Choose English because Pidgin no go take you anywhere/ nothing

BENJAMIN: I enter bus eh? I enter bus. One guy dey abuse conductor. *You tink say I no go school? Tink say I no go school?* Conductor say *If you go school, spell book.* The man look conductor and say *B U K, Buk.*

MUSA: *(Laughs.)*

BENJAMIN: You know wetin conductor talk? Conductor talk say… *Sorry, very good, very good, enter bus!*

SAMUEL & MUSA: *(Bigger laugh.)*

BENJAMIN: You see Pidgin makes life interesting! That's the thing.

SAMUEL: My father said it was banned in school?

BENJAMIN: Yes! So pidgin became language of rebellion.

MUSA: If Pidgin die, e go reduce harmony for Nigeria?

BENJAMIN: Yes oh! Because English no get that vibrancy, that tempo, that bond.

MUSA: So I should write a Pidgin-English dictionary?

BENJAMIN: Now you're talking! Five hundred languages for Naija, only Pidgin unite us. If that one disappear, problems! You know?

SCENE 5

KAMPALA // CHARACTERS:

SIMON – Ugandan. Early 30s

BRIAN – Ugandan. Early 30s

PAUL – Ugandan. Early 40s

// 10:45. A small two-chair barber shop in a shopping mall. There's a sofa beside the barber's chairs. SIMON cuts BRIAN.

BRIAN: You want to hear a joke?

   (Beat.)

BRIAN: Is that a yes?

   (Beat.)

BRIAN: Okay. A Muganda man, Munyankole and Acholi man are having drinks in a bar. Flies are buzzing all over the place… Bzzzz plop! One fly land in the Baganda/ man

SIMON: I don't want to hear.

BRIAN: You're still angry?

SIMON: You are always late! It has knock-on effects.

BRIAN: I don't knock on any effects.

SIMON: Because I haven't finished doing you and a client always comes around this/ time

   // PAUL storms in angrily.

SIMON: You see? If you came on time, I would be/ ready

PAUL: Look at my neck!

SIMON: Eh?

PAUL: Look at my neck!

SIMON: Paul, don't shout. What is/ the matter

25

PAUL: Look at my neck!

BRIAN: He talks to you like this?

PAUL: Look what you did to me last week!

SIMON: I didn't do/ anything

SIMON: What is it?

PAUL: In-growing hair. Look!

SIMON: Sit down.

// SIMON leans in.

SIMON: You've been touching it.

PAUL: No.

SIMON: This is what happens when you touch it.

PAUL: No.

SIMON: I'm a professional/ I never

PAUL: Just look at how/ ugly it is. You are a terrorist of neck.

SIMON: It's not what was happening/ before before

PAUL: When you touch it, when you touch/ it this is

BRIAN: Speak one at a time!

PAUL: Thank you! When you cut but don't wash, hair will start growing in, but when you clean thoroughly, pores are open, hair grows out. Last week you had no water in your shop / and could not wash

SIMON: So you don't shower when you get home?

PAUL: Skin replenish as I'm driving home. If you find open pore here, forty-five minutes later, it's closed.

SIMON: Do you live forty-six minutes away?

BRIAN Laughs.

PAUL: It wasn't happening before.

SIMON: Because you touch it!

PAUL: I don't touch myself.

SIMON: The more you disturb them, the more they disturb you!

PAUL: I don't disturb myself! / Nothing can make me

SIMON: Let me work!

// SIMON leans closer, intimately into PAUL, tending to his neck.

SIMON: You're not looking after your skin. You don't love it.

(Beat.)

PAUL: Nobody loves my skin more than me.

(Beat.)

SIMON: When you're bored you touch it, or you allow women to touch it.

PAUL: I don't believe in that kind of love.

SIMON & BRIAN laughs.

(Beat.)

SIMON: It's gone.

PAUL: Mmm.

SIMON: The swelling will go, it will be nice and smooth again.

PAUL: Thank you.

(Beat.)

BRIAN: When is the match?

SIMON: Kick off is two thirty, eleven thirty GMT.

BRIAN: Can't wait! Mirror.

(Beat.)

PAUL: Are you new? Never seen you here before.

SIMON: This man? *(Kisses teeth.)* He just calls me anytime, *I'm coming,* then arrives late!

BRIAN: I have legitimate reason.

SIMON: Always legitimate reason! What now?

BRIAN: Someone stole my cow.

SIMON: You must think I'm an idiot. I'll cut off your head with these clippers.

BRIAN: I'm serious, the village court case overran! Three and half hours!

SIMON: Were you shouting over the elders eh? You should just shush and listen.

BRIAN: I listened, but it's that my neighbour, it's him/ that stole

SIMON: Paul, every time, he is accusing his neighbour, who is a gay, about something. Does he personally target you? Come to shag among your plantains?!

PAUL laughs.

BRIAN: They say he wants to marry his gay lover. He stole my cow for dowry!

SIMON: Ridiculous! He needs at least ten! What will one do?

BRIAN: Why are you defending the gay?! This is not natural to Uganda.

SIMON: It's happening everywhere, so it's natural it'll happen here! Kwame who visited last week? That Ghanian businessman? He just settled in London, I wanted to do business with him but he says Ugandan exports face discrimination because we're attacking the gay, so now it's bad for business. Just grow up! Leave the gay alone, it's not your problem.

BRIAN: He stole my cow so it's my problem!

(Beat.)

Which business did you want to do with Kwame?

SIMON: Ancient secret hair formula.

PAUL: Secret formula?

SIMON: Passed from generation to generation. My mother makes it. Only 300,000 shillings. Just put some, hair will grow back.

BRIAN: Why don't you give me small to try. If it works, I give you all the money.

SIMON: *(Kisses teeth.)* You're not serious.

PAUL & BRIAN laugh.

SIMON: You don't think a man's love is worth one sick cow? It will die anyway, let him have it.

BRIAN: Stealing is stealing.

SIMON: Love makes you do crazy things eh? Ask Paul how much dowry he paid.

BRIAN: How much?

PAUL: Sixty cows.

ALL: *(Except PAUL.)* Sixty cows!

PAUL: *(Laughs.)* Us Baganda don't usually pay, but I wanted to.

SIMON: Brian, how many cows did you pay for your wife?

(Beat.)

BRIAN: I cannot moneyterise her.

SIMON & PAUL laugh.

BRIAN: She is worth more than anything! *(Laughing.)* Stop laughing… I'm being serious!

SCENE 6

LONDON // CHARACTERS:

SAMUEL – British & Nigerian & Pidgin. Early 20s.

EMMANUEL – Nigerian. Early 40s.

WINSTON – Caribbean. Early 30s.

MUHAMMED – Nigerian. Mid to late 30s.

TANAKA – British & Zimbabwe. Early 20s

// 11:00. Do For Love by 2pac plays. MUHAMMED has just arrived.

MUHAMMED: The things is, if you don't have a good job and a white woman and a black woman both like you, I'll chose the white woman. Two reasons. One, no dowry!

ALL: *(Laugh.)*

MUHAMMED: Two, the white woman can do anything if she loves you, but black woman, won't happen. She'd like to but when she tells her mum, *How long have you known him? Is he Nigerian? They're criminals oh! Eritreans don't like black people. Zimbabweans and Mugabe?* Her family won't allow it! A white woman, even if her people don't like you, will follow her heart.

EMMANUEL: They can't control her?

MUHAMMED: No! But still eh, I consider myself a proper black man.

EMMANUEL: You must have a black woman?

MUHAMMED: Yes!

TANAKA: You just contradicted yourself.

MUHAMMED: No, it's not that simple. I'll tell you a story. When I first came, ten years ago, one of my boys told me

Come to a club, one woman there likes you. Really? Is she black or white? He refused to tell me.

WINSTON: Good

MUHAMMED: Said I was racist.

TANAKA: Was she black or white?

MUHAMMED: Ah ah? I'm telling story!

EMMANUEL: Calm down!

MUHAMMED: So I go there, music is loud, people dancing, my friend points out one white girl. I greet her and I didn't know she's been watching me for ages! She order my favourite drink, two cans of RedBull– I'm Muslim, I don't drink. I wanted to pay and you know what? She said *No No No* She will buy the drinks. I said *Wow!* It has never happened before; woman pay for my shit! I'm loving this!

TANAKA: *(Laughs.)*

MUHAMMED: It was time to go, she ask where I live. *Five minutes down the road.* She said *Let's buy drinks on the way,* and paid as well! My friends, I was impressed. You wonder why they say white people are mean... and I started changing myself, you know.

ALL: Mmm

MUHAMMED: So she ask *Am I going out the next day?* I say *I'm not.* We got home, finish eating, shag, two, three times.

// ALL express their disbelief.

MUHAMMED: Don't blaspheme in this barber shop. You know what they call me? You know what they call me?

ALL: What?

MUHAMMED: Mr Lover Lover.

ALL: *(Laugh.)*

MUHAMMED: Around eight in the morning, this Jamaican girl I met when I was doing security called me, *Where are you?...* and I like that Jamaican girl well well!

TANAKA: Trouble!

WINSTON: Leave my people alone!

MUHAMMED: *(Laughs.)* I been wanting her for ages. I said I'm home. She said *Can we meet? Come to Walworth Road.* I sent a text message to my friend to act as if he just landed at Gatwick Airport so I'll come pick him up. I put the phone on loudspeaker: *Are you in Gatwick now?* He said *Ahhh yeah yeah* and the girl started looking at me. I said babes I have to pick up my friend at the airpot you know how it is babes. And you know what she said to me?

ALL: What?!

MUHAMMED: She said *I thought you weren't going out? That's why I never trust black people!*

ALL: What?!

MUHAMMED: Believe you me, that's what she said. I was feeling a little guilty, but after she said that, I didn't care! No way I'll let the other girl down.

(Beat.)

TANAKA: Jamaican... black right?

MUHAMMED: I liked her.

TANAKA: Though she's not white?

MUHAMMED: Yes! But you know, I should've stayed home, because when I went out, I spent more money!

ALL save TANAKA: *(Laugh.)*

MUHAMMED: Whites don't like us, but I'm not like Emmanuel here who only dates black women.

EMMANUEL: Don't involve me oh, Belinda my wife is brilliant, I'm happily married.

MUHAMMED: Happy marriage? No such thing.

ALL save TANAKA: *(Laugh.)*

WINSTON: You're contradicting yourself again.

TANAKA: Yeah, you just/ said that

MUHAMMED: I know what I said ah! Are you my psychiatrist? I'm saying I prefer white women but can date any race, because life is crazy.

TANAKA: YOU are crazy.

// TANAKA squares up to MUHAMMED.

MUHAMMED: Small boy, watch your mouth.

TANAKA: You're mad. Ignorant, foolish.

MUHAMMED: Say it again.

EMMANUEL: Hey! Calm down, this is a space for talking.

TANAKA: You're mixing culture with race and can't tell the difference! A black British woman will follow her heart just like a white British.

WINSTON: Besides, if y'na have adequate employment, none a dem choose you!

ALL: *(Laugh.)*

MUHAMMED: Winston! They will chose me.

WINSTON: Need to sit yourself down bwoy and listen.

// SAMUEL enters from the backroom.

SAMUEL: Muhammed! I thought they deported you!

ALL: *(Laugh.)*

MUHAMMED: Donald Trump and Theresa May can't catch me. That's why I always have skin cuts, sleek, I'm too fast! How body? Wetin dey?

SAMUEL: I'm okay man. Trim?

MUHAMMED: Eight pounds as usual?

33

SAMUEL: Of course.

MUHAMMED: My guy.

SAMUEL: Sitdon there, I dey come.

// SAMUEL for the door.

EMMANUEL: Where you going?

SAMUEL: Eleven o'clock. I'm on my break.

EMMANUEL: We don't have scheduled breaks.

SAMUEL: *(Laughs.)*

EMMANUEL: What's funny?

SAMUEL: You're asking where I am going?

EMMANUEL: You have a client.

SAMUEL: Didn't make an appointment.

EMMANUEL: So?

SAMUEL: Listen. You cut your hair, I'll cut mine.

EMMANUEL: All I'm saying/ is maybe you

SAMUEL: Fuck what you're saying!/

WINSTON: Samuel!

EMMANUEL: You can't/ just leave

SAMUEL: None your business where I go!

MUHAMMED: No, I can wait. No problem.

SAMUEL: Can't tell me what to do/ who are

EMMANUEL: I wasn't/ telling you what

SAMUEL: You're not my Dad yeah?

WINSTON: Sam!

SAMUEL: Don't care how much you stand there in his place, you'll never be half the man/ he is

WINSTON: Sam! Samuel!

// SAMUEL exits. WINSTON walks after him. EMMANUEL stops WINSTON.

(Beat.)

TANAKA: So... yeah... Who is in the starting line up?

// ALL: Look intensely at the screen.

MUHAMMED: Suarez is there?

WINSTON: Yeah.

MUHAMMED: I don't like him.

WINSTON: Why?

MUHAMMED: Racist. When he was at Liverpool he called Evra a negro.

EMMANUEL: No, he suffered racism too! They banned him *because* he is South American, because when John Terry did it to Anton Ferdinand, everyone rushed to his defence.

MUHAMMED: That's because Terry was from this country, captain of England team, and a white man. He was untouchable... both of them, racist.

EMMANUEL: No, Suarez also said he didn't mean it like that. Where he's from, *Negro* means black.

MUHAMMED: Uncle Emmanuel, he mean't it! When you pinch someone like this and say *Negro*... What's that mean?

WINSTON: That true you na.

MUHAMMED: And in the last World Cup, he was biting people. You can't defend him.

EMMANUEL: Okay, I see your point.

MUHAMMED: Evra said as an African, being called *Negro* hurts, and the FA were saying he should move on. Move where?! Especially when every week, fans are chanting *monkey, nigger!*

WINSTON: But everyone uses it now. Just de other day, me a see two white yout, over dere on de high street, broad daylight, singing dat song *Ma Nigga Ma Nigga*. Maybe we na help tings? Rap music, nigger this, nigger that.

TANAKA: Nigger is not bad though.

MUHAMMED: No!

EMMANUEL: It's not about the word, it's the context in which it's used and who uses it.

WINSTON: If a white man uses it you'll get offended?

TANAKA: Yeah, because a black man won't use it as a derogative term.

MUHAMMED: Still No! Because, it started with the white man abusing the black man.

TANAKA: No, it started with us! *Negus* is what ancient Ethiopians called regional kings, yes. Then *Negra/Nigre/ Negro* is latin and Spanish for Black, a colour, not offensive and offence depends where you are anyway. In South Africa, call a black man *Kaffir*, see what happen. That's worse / than any

MUHAMMED: No! Look at it from slavery, it was used to insult. Nigre is black. Necro means death. 'Black Death'. That's what they called us!

EMMANUEL: Slavery was bad, much worse than holocaust even. Holocaust was six million, terrible eh, slavery, thirty million Africans died! Minimum, so to reclaim the word is saying we're moving past slavery.

TANAKA: And 2Pac says there's a difference between N.I.G.G.A and N.I.G.G.E.R/

MUHAMMED: What did you say?

TANAKA: 2Pac says

MUHAMMED: *(to EMMANUEL)* Uncle where did you get this boy from? *(To TANAKA)* Whether you change the spelling, GGA or GGER, it means the same thing! 2face, 2Pac, whatever! Shit in any language smells like shit! ! Am I wrong? Am I wrong?

ALL: *(Laugh.)*

EMMANUEL: Oya, the cup final is starting!

// EMMANUEL increases the volume. A whistle blows.

ALL: *(Save EMMANUEL.)* Up Chelsea! Come on!

SCENE 7

JOBURG // CHARACTERS:

FABRICE – Cameroon. Early 20s.

SHONI – South African. Early 30s.

SIMPHIWE – South African. 40s.

// 12:00. Roadside barber shop. The match is on the radio. FABRICE cuts SHONI's beard, SIMPHIWE is drinking a can of beer.

FABRICE: Back home in Cameroon, I wanted to be a tabloid journalist too but got in trouble for writing satire about Goodluck Jonathan.

SHONI: *(Laughs.)* He was the most abused president in the world.

SIMPHIWE: We did worse to President Zuma, booed him at Mandela's ceremony but cheered for Goodluck.

SHONI: He has the most ridiculous name though.

FABRICE: Specially if you are sarcastic. *Want to save Nigeria? Goodluck!*

SIMPHIWE: Things must have been tough for his family. You know how black people give names. When things are good, names are good. If it's tough/ things are

SHONI: It's so true! First born in my family was Themba, it means/

FABRICE: I know this!... er/

SIMPHIWE: Faith!

FABRICE: Ah! I knew it.

SHONI: Second was Langa,

FABRICE: Sunshine!

SHONI: Third born is Njabulo

FABRICE: Happiness!

SHONI: Yah! Your knowledge of our language is growing! Life got hard after the fourth middle child, me. Shonisani...

FABRICE: Er... I don't know this one...

SHONI: It means expectations, good or bad. My parents literally did not know what the fuck would happen next. Things went downhill after... names changed... Lindani!

FABRICE: Patience!

SHONI: Bhehezela!

FABRICE: Endurance!

SHONI: And the last Nkosi-Sisize,

FABRICE: God help us!

SHONI & FABRICE: *(Laughs.)*

SHONI: Wait wait shhhh...

// They listen as a goal is scored.

SHONI & FABRICE: Goooooooal! Up Chelsea! One – Nil Chelsea!

SIMPHIWE: Goal.

SHONI: If we win, me and my date are drinking and dancing tonight, fuck dinner.

SIMPHIWE: Yoh! You got so drunk last night!

FABRICE: That surprised me when I came here from Cameroon. You guys can drink!

SIMPHIWE: It's because of those vineyards, they made us...

// SIMPHIWE stares at his drink.

(Beat.)

FABRICE: Is the beard okay now?

SHONI: Cut it down more please. I want to look like a superstar rapper.

FABRICE: *(Laughs.)* You have grey hair. I can dye it?

SIMPHIWE: That's like women getting extensions! Hell no! In the heat of passion, you cannot pull her hair!

FABRICE: Why would you do that to a woman? In my opinion, never do that.

SIMPHIWE: You're young, your opinion does not matter.

(Beat.)

SHONI: *(Laughs.)* One comedian said black women get away with murder because DNA from their hair will be traced to a bald woman in India!

SIMPHIWE & FABRICE: *(Laugh.)*

// The radio plays.

FABRICE: I didn't like Chelsea till that legendary match against Byern Munich. So impressive!

(Beat.)

When Nigeria beat Burkina Faso in the African Cup of Nations, my friend Wole in London went around making everyone honorary Nigerians. He was so happy!

(Beat.)

Shoni, you're beginning to look like a rapper, gonna be the coolest nigga in the club.

FABRICE: Don't say Nigga. It's offensive.

SHONI: Huh? *Kaffir!* That's offensive! Because Afrikaners called us that; it's about power.

SIMPHIWE: *(Laughs.)* You know in school I had power over them? Charged white kids to call me Kaffir.

SHONI: What?!

SIMPHIWE: *(Laughing.)* Yes! I'd be like… *For one rand you can call me one time, for two rand, call me two times.* Headmaster called me into his office and asked why. I said *They wanna*

*call me that. I know, they wanna call me that. They know, I
know, they wanna call me that so/ why not*

SHONI: I'd never have done that. I moved to the suburbs,
white-people area, and they used it everyday, assaulted
my mother.

FABRICE: Eish! How?

SHONI: They beat up my cousin, he called her, they beat her
too shouting *Kaffir Bitch!* She wanted to move but my Dad
said *Fuck No! Not going anywhere.*

FABRICE: He wanted to stand and fight like a man!

SIMPHIWE: A real man avoids fights.

SHONI: What you saying about my father?

SIMPHIWE: I… nothing Shoni.

(Beat.)

// They listen as Suarez scores a goal.

SHONI & FABRICE: Nooo!

FABRICE: Bastard.

(Beat.)

SHONI: Can't believe you. Dollar to call you kaffir? Pathetic.
They probably think that's how much we're worth.

SIMPHIWE: I… It was a long time ago.

FABRICE: Nigger, Kaffir, don't like any.

(Beat.)

SHONI: Now more of them are coming, Europeans, investing
in our country. I'll take their cash. Will my views about
them change? No!

FABRICE: We should invest in our own country.

SHONI: Europe is so poor now… You know he wanted to go
to Wales?

SIMPHIWE: A while ago.

SHONI: Just last month! He said *I want to go to Wales and work.*

SIMPHIWE: Because of my son.

SHONI: Your son is an actor in London! I'm like *Why you wanna go when they're all coming here?*

FABRICE: We must put visa restrictions on them!

SHONI: They chase us out of Europe, treat us all the same.

FABRICE: They should treat you differently?

SHONI: Especially me. People say I don't look South African.

FABRICE: What d'you mean?

SHONI: Africans all look different. Ethiopians, West, East/ Africans

FABRICE: I know, how are you different from South Africans?

SHONI: I'll tell you now… look, look… see how handsome I am?

FABRICE: *(Laughs.)* I'm finished.

// FABRICE brushes SHONI with a feather duster.

SHONI: Only on the continent! Cleaning by feather duster.

SIMPHIWE: What kind of feathers are these?

(Beat.)

I want a swan-feather duster; I'm a king and I love my skin.

SHONI: A king?

SIMPHIWE: Yes

SHONI: Thought you were a Kaffir?

SCENE 8

LONDON // CHARACTERS:

SAMUEL – British & Nigerian & Pidgin. Early 20s.

WINSTON – Caribbean. Early 30s.

EMMANUEL – Nigerian. Early 40s.

OHENE – Ghanaian. Late 40s.

TANAKA – British & Zimbabwe. Early 20s.

WOLE – Nigerian. Mid 30s.

// 12:45 SAMUEL runs in, WINSTON cuts OHENE's hair. The match is on.

SAMUEL: Still two all?

TANAKA: Yeah. Seven minutes to go.

   (Beat.)

SAMUEL: You're letting him cut your hair?

OHENE: Why not?

SAMUEL: Don't trust him oh.

OHENE: What's he done?

SAMUEL: I'm telling you…

OHENE: What?

SAMUEL: Last week, his birthday eh/

WINSTON: *(Laugh.)*

SAMUEL: He got a bottle of rum/ big, huge

WINSTON: Stop going on about this… me never buy it/ it was given to me.

SAMUEL: Came with rum, put it on the table for everyone to see. I'm thinking *Tonight I'm gonna drink! It's my boy's*

43

birthday. The guy finished work, put the rum in his bag and left!

WINSTON: Ya shoulda buy me one.

SAMUEL: It was your birthday!

WINSTON: Exactly, you buy me one!

SAMUEL: You're the host, you provide drinks!

WINSTON: Not how Jamaicans do it. It was a present, given to me!

OHENE: Who gave you?

(Beat.)

WINSTON: Melissa.

SAMUEL: What!? She bribed you to leave her alone and you were still bugging her last night?

ALL: *(Laugh.)*

WINSTON: To be honest, it never cross my mind.

SAMUEL: How did it not cross your mind?

WINSTON: Africans na drink!

ALL: Rubbish.

WINSTON: It's true. Yu not interested. How many of you go pub? Right! Least there're couple Jamaican ones. But Africans, nothing! That's why you fill up the barber shop. This is your pub. Yu na drink!

TANAKA: No, in South Africa, in the vineyards, white farmers paid coloureds and blacks barrels of wine instead of money. Generations later, they're still pissed.

WINSTON: That's a special case but generally. Africans na drink.

SAMUEL: Me, personally, I smoke weed.

ALL: *(React.)*

44

OHENE: You Fela Kuti followers have come again!

SAMUEL: It helps me relax! But what's wrong with Fela? He was a hero to Africa so/ I see no problem

OHENE: Rubbish! Even Nigerians didn't like him.

ALL: No!!!!

OHENE: Older generations say Fela sang against corruption, yet smoked half the weed in Lagos!

ALL: *(Laugh.)*

OHENE: Only recently people started celebrating him, Fela Festivals everywhere! Have you asked why?

TANAKA: His music!

OHENE: Small boy, you don't know anything.

WINSTON: Why?

OHENE: The west embraced him!

WINSTON: The west?

OHENE: The west!

SAMUEL: Have to stop giving white people credit for black achievements.

OHENE: I said *West* not *White*.

SAMUEL: It's the same thing!

OHENE: No *we* are the west! Now our young people want to smoke, make music, instead of getting proper jobs.

TANAKA: I'm a young person and/ there are opportunities in music to do bigger things

OHENE: You're a young person so your opinion does not matter.

ALL: *(Laugh.)*

TANAKA: Wait till we run Africa, we'll show you how it's done.

OHENE: You want to save Africa? *Goodluck!*

SAMUEL: People liked Fela because he told the truth. Weed is another issue.

OHENE: You can't divorce a man from his actions. Same thing with these rich pastors preaching penitent life but have private jets. Christianity is the biggest business in Africa.

TANAKA: (*Sigh.*) Money is the root of all evil.

OHENE: Small boy! You've come again.

WINSTON: Sorry landlord, cyan't pay my rent. Money is the root of all evil.

ALL: (*Laugh.*)

WOLE: You can't criticise pastors for making cash. After all, they're just doing what they were taught. There's that saying eh… *When they came, we had the land and they had the Bible. They taught us to pray with our eyes closed. When we opened them, they had the land and we had*

ALL: *The Bible!*

WOLE: Christianity has always been about money. Now Africans are making the cash, suddenly it is a problem.

OHENE: When you run Africa will you ban religion? Can you?

WINSTON: All money is dirty money, what we do cleans it up.

// ALL watch football.

ALL: Look… look… Goal!!

// EMMANUEL's phone beeps.

// TANAKA goes to EMMANUEL who cuts WOLE's hair.

TANAKA: They well deserved that!

WOLE: Those black guys are central to the attacking team.

SAMUEL: Who is that?

EMMANUEL: Nobody.

SAMUEL: Nobody?

EMMANUEL: Nobody... It's my business.

WOLE: ENTER! That goal was effortless.

EMMANUEL: They better watch their back. Suarez will bite them now.

WOLE: All four of them played in the African Cup of Nations Uncle Emmanuel, all of them, so talented! I couldn't believe when we won! I was so happy, I went round making everyone honorary Nigerians. It's not often we have reasons to be proud of our country, because that country is... problems! You know, if I had power, everyone over forty-five in government, I will sack, corrupt or not.

EMMANUEL: Even me?

WOLE: No offence. Either that or young people should rise up.

EMMANUEL: They will get squashed! That country is under military rule really, even if there was a coup, they'll just bribe the guys at the door, *Ah ah, haba, go and sit down jor, woz wrong wit you? Take dis now, take dis.* Money talks too much.

TANAKA: It's the root of all evil.

WOLE: The only upside: it forces one to enterprise. My whole family have their businesses. No job seekers allowance.

TANAKA: See! Welfare creates a safety net that makes people complacent here.

OHENE: Our young politician strikes again!

// ALL look at the screen as a goal is missed.

ALL: Ohhhh!

SAMUEL: What is the keeper doing?

WINSTON: Sleeping?

(Beat.)

OHENE: Remember that Welcome to Lagos documentary?

SAMUEL: Typical BBC, go to the slums to film a documentary on Lagos.

TANAKA: That's like coming to London and filming an estate in Peckham.

EMMANUEL: I live in an estate in Peckham.

TANAKA: *(Laughs.)*

EMMANUEL: I'll cut your head off with this clipper.

WOLE: Sorry, I mean those floating slums are real but it's not all of Lagos. You know they're building floating schools!

TANAKA: Amazing… see Nigerians make it happen! Not like Ghanaians.

OHENE: Hey!

EMMANUEL: My wife is Ghanaian.

WOLE: What kind of man are you?

SAMUEL: Traitor to your own race!

TANAKA: *(Laughs.)*

// EMMANUEL's phone beeps.

ALL: Pass it!

SAMUEL: Who is that?

EMMANUEL: Nobody!

SAMUEL: Same nobody from before?

EMMANUEL: A ah?!

ALL: Pass it! Aahhhhhh!

WOLE: He should have curved it now!

OHENE: Why did he try to lob the keeper, it was open!

WINSTON: Geedy!

OHENE: Idiot. He's getting too much money!

TANAKA: He should give me some.

WINSTON: *(Laughs.)* Fe what?

TANAKA: For being a fan!

WINSTON: What ya talk 'bout?

TANAKA: For supporting them.

WOLE: There's difference between a fan and a supporter.

EMMANUEL: What? Hey hey hey!

// EMMANUEL draws attention to the match.

ALL: Oooh!!!

EMMANUEL: What's the difference?

WOLE: What?

EMMANUEL: Between fan and supporter.

WOLE: So… a supporter just watches match, team loose, he's
disappointed, that's all. But a fan will be sad, you no fit
talk to am, depressed, as if someone died.

ALL: *(Laugh.)*

WOLE: A supporter has a shirt, maybe a cap. A fan will have
the full away kit, wear it the whole day.

ALL: *(Laugh.)*

WOLE: A supporter knows the team motto: *You'll never walk
alone.* A fan engraves it on his wife's wedding ring! *Honey,
You'll never walk alone.*

ALL: *(Laugh.)*

// ALL turn to the screen as another goal is missed.

ALL: Oooh!

EMMANUEL: Just clipped the top left!

WINSTON: What's the keeper doing?

EMMANUEL: We'll get you next time.

SAMUEL: You're three-two down, minutes left. You don't have a fucking chance mate. *We'll get you next time?* Not a fucking chance/ mate. You couldn't score

WINSTON: Sam!

SAMUEL: What?

WINSTON: Too much disrespect. Ya can't talk to him like that in front of people.

EMMANUEL: Heeeeey, I can fight my own battles. He's just a bit excited.

(Beat.)

// EMMANUEL makes for the door.

SAMUEL: Where you going?

EMMANUEL: Out.

ALL: Ey!

SAMUEL: You're working.

EMMANUEL: Don't have clients.

ALL: Ey!

SAMUEL: You can't just leave.

EMMANUEL: This is my shop.

ALL: Ey!

SAMUEL: What's more important than this? Than here?

EMMANUEL: Get out of my way.

ALL: Ey!

SAMUEL: Uncle? Emmanuel! Where are you going?

ALL: Goal!!!

// The final whistle. The match finishes. All surround and taunt
EMMANUEL chanting:

Them they loose oh! One by one.

Them they loose oh! One by one.

Them they loose oh! One by one.

Them they loose oh! One by one!

SAMUEL: Take the defeat like a man.

// WOLE & TANAKA block his path.

SAMUEL: Who you gonna meet?

// EMMANUEL angrily slams his bag on the floor. A moment of
stillness. They part, EMMANUEL lifts his bag, walks through them.

// EMMANUEL leaves.

SCENE 9

HARARE // CHARACTERS:

TINASHE – Zimbabwean. Early 20s.

DWAIN – Zimbabwean. Mid 30s.

// 15:00 A ceiling fan swirls above. Bob Marley's One Love plays. TINASHE pours cream from a giant tub into smaller bottles. He doesn't have enough space on the tables, we laugh as he creates a mess of things. DWAIN enters.

DWAIN: Did you watch the match? We destroyed Barcelona!

TINASHE: Ah! Dwain! Just the man I'm looking for.

DWAIN: Oooh, what's all this?

TINASHE: New delivery straight from Kampala! Anti-balding cream made with local Ugandan herbs. Ancient formula.

DWAIN: Are you trying to sell me one?

TINASHE: Huh?

DWAIN: Am I balding? Why am I the man you're looking for?

TINASHE: *(Laughs.)* No. My cousin Tanaka is moving back from London on Wednesday. I'm trying to prepare him for the change, and you just moved back too.

DWAIN: Does he have a British passport? What's his job?

TINASHE: Ya British passport. He writes about politics a bit.

DWAIN: Yo! vaMugabe doesn't like people from the west. They always lying about him. If he says he is a writer, he won't get past the border.

TINASHE: *(Laughs.)* That's exactly the kinda stuff I need!

DWAIN: Okay. But haircut? On the house?

TINASHE: Yeah.

52

DWAIN: So listen, I wanted to talk about your party anyway.

// DWAIN sits by radio and tunes into Chimurenga music.

TINASHE: I bet you don't have parties in Joburg… is that why you left and came back to Harare?

DWAIN: *(Laughs.)* I came back because our music industry has grown. I wanted to do hip-hop when I was twenty-one but there were no spaces, so I left. Now, things have changed. More cash, more venues, and now we play local music! I play the same gigs here that I did in Joburg. Here, I make more. Don't know how long it's gonna last, but for now…

TINASHE: It's good?

DWAIN: Ya! So much music! But the world doesn't know.

TINASHE: Why?

DWAIN: Because Zimbabwe is bashed by media outside, because vaMugabe took land from white people.

TINASHE: To a returnee, how d'you explain what happened?

DWAIN: We took back our land.

(Beat.)

TINASHE: That's it?

DWAIN: *(Laughs.)* Plain and simple.

TINASHE: People were killed.

DWAIN: Yah.

TINASHE: White people.

DWAIN: So?

(Beat.)

TINASHE: Tanaka has white friends. They believe/ that

DWAIN: White *and* Black people died. Both. We wanted our land back and got it! See, we are natural farmers. Before, most of us owned land and our food came from that land.

53

THIS is our culture, like Kenyans are cattle herders, that's their culture. And yes, you know, our crops failed; but after generations without our land there were bound to be teething problems you know, yet they were ridiculing us and vaMugabe.

TINASHE: My mother told me.

DWAIN: VaMugabe has eight degrees and they think he is stupid. He is struggling on the global stage, that's why I'm making Chimurenga music. Chimurenga means struggle/ and I want

TINASHE: (*Sigh.*) I know Dwain. You tell everyone.

DWAIN: At your party, you weren't playing Chimurenga.

TINASHE: It wasn't the right vibe.

DWAIN: If you played it, it would have become the vibe. We have to support each other. You really disappointed me, your party was shit! Young people should play our own music. My songs are all about/ our attempts

TINASHE: We can play what we want!

DWAIN: We should play who we are.

// TINASHE turns off the radio.

TINASHE: At the party, people were asking *who's the old guy hassling djs, telling them what to play.* If you don't like the music, go!

// DWAIN pulls away sharply

DWAIN: I'm trying to restore national identity / to our

TINASHE: By what?! By plying us with your shit songs? Pretending to care? You left Dwain! You left! When things got tough, you left. Things are better, you've come back, acting like you care, wanna tell us who we are? We don't want your dictatorship, Mugabe is enough!

DWAIN: Before I left young people would never talk to elders like this.

TINASHE: The older a man get, the faster he could run as a boy.

// DWAIN stands up.

DWAIN: I don't have to listen to this. There're other barbers/ who won't insult

TINASHE: Go! It's just three o'clock! More clients will come! Don't need your money!

// DWAIN storms off.

TINASHE: It was a free hair cut anyway!

SCENE 10

SAMUEL – British & Nigerian & Pidgin. Early 20s.

EMMANUEL – Nigerian. Early 40s.

SIZWE – Zimbabwean. Early 50s.

TANAKA – British & Zimbabwe. Early 20s.

// 16:00 SAMUEL is cutting SIZWE'S hair. TANAKA listens to their conversation.

SIZWE: When I was young in Zimbabwe, my uncle was a barber, travelled from village to village on a bicycle, up mountains, down hills, leg muscles like iron! When he arrived, the kids would shout *The Barber! The Barber! The Barber is here!* He cut ten villages in one day, his family wouldn't see him for a month! And he didn't have electric razors: manual clippers! His hands were tough! And boy, we had headaches after a haircut. Sometimes the clippers were rusty; not actually cutting hair, but pulling it out. I was twelve when I first felt an electric razor, fell asleep in the chair; it was so soothing. My uncle slapped me across the back of the neck. I jumped out of my skin.

SAMUEL: Ten villages? In one day?

SIZWE: You don't believe me?

SAMUEL: There's a saying: the older a man gets, the faster he could run as a boy.

SIZWE: Is it your policy to insult clients?

TANAKA: *(Laughs.)* Just don't pay him!

SAMUEL: *(Laughs.)* I'm finished sir.

SIZWE: Thank you Samuel.

SAMUEL: I'll get your coat.

// SAMUEL goes to get SIZWE's coat and returns.

SIZWE: Erm… I seem to be low on cash.

TANAKA: Oh, I can lend/ you some

SIZWE: No… It's fine/ I can just

SAMUEL: Just pay next time. We have to look after our old men.

SIZWE: *(Laughs.)* Shut your mouth before I show you something.

> *(Beat.)*

Thank you. *(To TANAKA.)* And safe travels.

TANAKA: Thank you sir.

// SIZWE is leaving as EMMANUEL enters.

SAMUEL: Did you want a cut?

TANAKA: Er… Yeah. Where's Winston?

SAMUEL: Did you make an appointment?

TANAKA: Yeah, three hours ago.

SAMUEL: He is out, he has a four o'clock home client.

TANAKA: Right.

EMMANUEL: My friend. *(Gestures to his chair.)*

SAMUEL: I'd watch him if I was you.

TANAKA: What?

SAMUEL: Man has a history of violence and stealing people's business / if he

EMMANUEL: Samuel.

SAMUEL: What?

> *(Beat.)*
>
> Three years to the day since went in, remember? And you can't even apologise.

(Beat.)

EMMANUEL: Whatever you feel happened, I think/ you should think

SAMUEL: Move man.

// SAMUEL leaves. EMMANUEL is silent, gestures again.

TANAKA: Winston cuts me.

EMMANUEL: I trained Winston. All the time you've been coming here, we've not spoken.

TANAKA: I always go to Winston.

EMMANUEL: I don't mind. Just an observation.

(Beat.)

TANAKA: Lower the sides and a shape up?

EMMANUEL: I know.

TANAKA: Same price?

EMMANUEL: Eight pounds.

(Beat.)

// TANAKA sits.

(Beat.)

TANAKA: What Sam said… a history of violence?

EMMANUEL: Let's just say I used to… communicate with my fists when I was young. I was someone else. I stopped when I started barbing, when Samuel was born. Both things can't exist in a man.

(Beat.)

TANAKA: Stealing people's business?

EMMANUEL: That's another conversation.

(Beat.)

TANAKA: You've known him for a while?

EMMANUEL: Yes. He's my best friend's boy.

TANAKA: His father started the shop?

EMMANUEL: He invested more than us, but we were three, Malachi, Elnathan and me. Young rascals. Your age. So similar, we had the same poster above our chairs.

TANAKA: *(Laughs.)*

EMMANUEL: Same dreams.

TANAKA: The others stopped cutting? Where are they?... Ouch!

EMMANUEL: When last did you wash or comb your hair? Come every week, I'll wash it for you.

TANAKA: I can't. This is the last haircut. Going to Zimbabwe on Wednesday.

EMMANUEL: Coming back?

TANAKA: Maybe... next February.

(Beat.)

EMMANUEL: So you are Mugabe's son.

TANAKA: *(Laughs.)*

EMMANUEL: I like the man.

TANAKA: *(Laughs nervously.)* We all do.

EMMANUEL: I really, really like the man.

TANAKA: Why?

EMMANUEL: What's not to like?

(Beat.)

I mean, I know what I hear about him.

TANAKA: What do you hear?

EMMANUEL: You know... stole elections, corrupt, ruthless, banned white people from owning land/ and

TANAKA: You don't think they are true?

EMMANUEL: Not everything you hear is true, and it depends on who's talking.

TANAKA: What do you really think of him?

(Beat.)

EMMANUEL: Really?... Mugabe acts like a man, he's a natural president. You agree?

TANAKA: I'm listening.

EMMANUEL: Also, more than 50% of Zimbabweans are okay in the home system.

TANAKA: You know how many Zimbabweans left the country because of what happened?

EMMANUEL: But you're going back.

TANAKA: Well, it's my home. We all want to be home don't we? Ultimately? I want to be part of it. We should paint Zimbabwe with colours other than Mugabe, and change how we talk about ourselves to each other and the rest of the world.

EMMANUEL: *(Laughs.)* You really want to be a politician?

TANAKA: No, I just... want... I don't know.

(Beat.)

EMMANUEL: The whole world insults him, horrible things, younger people not knowing what their talking, making embarrassing allegations, for years, yet he stays silent, holds his head high. It's not easy.

TANAKA: I... I understand.

EMMANUEL: Mmm hmm.

(Beat.)

TANAKA: Sorry... about the match, blocking your way/ I should not have

EMMANUEL: It's okay.

(Beat.)

TANAKA: This should last me a few weeks?

EMMANUEL: At least.

TANAKA: Thanks.

EMMANUEL: See you in February?

TANAKA: Hopefully not.

EMMANUEL: *(Laughs.)* Take care and Good luck!

TANAKA: Say goodbye to Winston for me.

SCENE 11

JOBURG // CHARACTERS:

ANDILE – South African. 30s/40s/50s.

SIMPHIWE – South African. Late 40s.

// 17:00 SIMPHIWE enters, still drinking and ANDILE greets him.

SIMPHIWE: Can I get a haircut?

ANDILE: You went to another barber didn't you?

> *(Beat.)*

> I trained Fabrice. We're a small community, we know each other.

SIMPHIWE: Well it's not my community, gossiping about/ clients behind

ANDILE: It used to be Simphiwe. You've lost your way.

> *(Beat.)*

> You know your father is looking for you?

SIMPHIWE: I'm going back to England soon.

ANDILE: See him first.

SIMPHIWE: NO.

ANDILE: He's changed, held a dinner during Mandela's funeral and sang. His voice moved us to tears.

SIMPHIWE: You don't know my father. Fuck him and Mandela! I don't need to…

> *(Beat.)*

> I ever tell you how I met my father for the first time? Want to know who he really is?

ANDILE: I know he was a travelling church singer, he was away a lot.

62

SIMPHIWE: Away? He had girlfriends everywhere, had one
    when he met my mother. Both fell pregnant at the same
    time. He went with the other one. My mother was too
    young so I lived with my grandparents. I could never
    get any information about him. I moved to London, got
    married, had a son but never stopped looking. Eventually
    when I was forty, I tracked him down and discovered I
    was the eldest of ten kids! Just one simple question I asked
    him... *How come you never came to look for me? You knew
    where I was...* Know what he said? He said *I thought you
    were gonna be another drunk rubbish, so didn't bother.*

    (Beat.)

ANDILE: Alcohol is in our blood. Generations of being paid
    only wine in those vineyards... but you beat it.

SIMPHIWE: Zero tolerance... until I found out his kids were
    starving because he spent all his money on drink, beating
    them and the wife. Next time I saw him, that same month,
    all he asked for was money. Not how I was, about my son,
    just money. I got so angry, I punched him.

ANDILE: He told me that.

SIMPHIWE: Started drinking when I got back to London. Wife
    threw me out of my own house.

ANDILE: Yoh!

SIMPHIWE: Haven't seen my son since he was six. My wife
    knew about my father, that I could do such things.

ANDILE: You're not like him Simphiwe.

SIMPHIWE: *(Laughs.)* We grow up to become our fathers. No.
    It's good she kicked me out.

    (Beat.)

ANDILE: You know anything about your son?

SIMPHIWE: Yah! I type his name in the internet every day. He is an actor, strong black man… doing wonderful things, even with my blood.

ANDILE: *Because* of your blood.

SIMPHIWE: No, it's his mother's.

ANDILE: And you're fine with this?

SIMPHIWE: Ya! He is already better than me.

(Beat.)

ANDILE: Are *you* fine Simphiwe?

(Beat.)

SIMPHIWE: I'm here. It's more than I can say for too many others.

(Beat.)

You know my grandparents worked tirelessly to get me through school. Money was so tight, I used to charge white kids to call me *Kaffir*, just so I could buy food.

ANDILE: Yoh!

SIMPHIWE: Like I said, fuck my father and Mandela.

ANDILE: The soil is still fresh on Mandela's grave!

SIMPHIWE: Winnie Mandela should have led this country! It was because of her he was freed. She said let's render South Africa ungovernable, fuck it up so whites have no choice but to back down. That's why they freed Mandela, and he let them off easily.

ANDILE: No. We had to forget the race thing, otherwise/ there will have been

SIMPHIWE: Otherwise what? Look at our society. The fact we never got to deal with it manifests in violence; men who rape children, beat women. If criminals hijack a car, they slit the driver's throat. We are still frustrated! Generations emasculated, called *boys* for centuries, taking it out on each other because we never got to get mad and say we were fucked around for 350 years and no one was held accountable.

ANDILE: TRC happened! Truth and reconciliation/commission

SIMPHIWE: Was a farce! A whole year of countless blacks coming forward saying my father was murdered, brother tortured, son mutilated. All the perpetrators had to do was admit it or apologise and most didn't even do that! They said *we were taking orders... in a war situation,* for us it was genocide.

ANDILE: What do you want? Official sympathy?

SIMPHIWE: All those official hypocrites that called him a terrorist, English Prime Minister David Cameron, Bill Clinton, came to his funeral. Fuck sympathy! It's time for whites to fucking pay! You know a recent survey showed forty percent of white South Africans don't think apartheid was wrong.

(Beat.)

This is the world we still live in. Mandela failed us. The balance of economic power is still with them in our own land! Am I wrong? You know there's a prophecy? The Night of Long Knives, when we take back our wealth, pangas flashing by moonlight. They're right to be afraid.

(Beat.)

ANDILE: You can't do nothing about Mandela, but your father wants to make amends.

SIMPHIWE: You're not listening. He... never said sorry.

(Beat.)

ANDILE: He wants to.

(Beat.)

Say the word, I'll set it up. You, him, here, now.

(Beat.)

Or I can give you a haircut first.

(Beat.)

What do you want to do?

SCENE 12

LONDON // CHARACTERS:

SAMUEL – British & Nigerian & Pidgin. Early 20s.

EMMANUEL – Nigerian. Early 40s.

WINSTON – Caribbean. Early 30s.

ELNATHAN – Nigerian. Early 40s.

// 18:00 EMMANUEL is talking with ELNATHAN.

ELNATHAN: So, there were two rivals, one tough lawman and a legendary smuggler. Throughout their careers, they had been fighting each other, from job to job, post to post, their paths always crossed.

EMMANUEL: Eh

ELNATHAN: One day that lawman was stationed at a border crossing and this smuggler had to pass to the next country to trade.

EMMANUEL: *(Laughs.)*

ELNATHAN: The lawman started rubbing his hands, *I will catch him today! He won't escape.* When the smuggler arrived, he told him, *Climb down from that camel! Now!* and he searched everything, every pocket, didn't find anything so he had to let him cross.

EMMANUEL: A ah?

ELNATHAN: Next month, same thing, *Get off that camel!* Searched everything, held the man in blazing heat for hours, no water, no shade. Found nothing, had to let him go.

EMMANUEL: Ah!

ELNATHAN: Third time, the lawman checked the camel's mouth, strip-searched the man on the road there, stood him there naked, even shined a torchlight up his nyash/

EMMANUEL: *(Laughs.)*

ELNATHAN: Didn't find anything. The lawman said *I know you are smuggling something.* Smuggler said *You didn't find nothing, have to let me go,* so he did. Years later when they retired. Lawman, standing outside his house, saw the old smuggler.

EMMANUEL: Ei!

ELNATHAN: Lawman invited him for a cup of tea. He said *All those years you were coming and going on the camels, I searched everything, even you, yet, nothing. But I KNOW you were smuggling something. What was it?*

EMMANUEL: What did he say?

ELNATHAN: The smuggler laughed! *All these years, you didn't know?* Lawman: *No! What was it? Tell me.* You know what he said?

EMMANUEL: What?

ELNATHAN: Camels!

EMMANUEL: *(Laughs.)*

ELNATHAN: He was smuggling camels! He didn't know!

EMMANUEL: *(Laughs.)* Elnathan! You and your mouth eh? Er… how is your nephew? Wallace?

// WINSTON enters.

You've not met Winston before? Winston, come and meet my friend.

WINSTON: Evening sir.

ELNATHAN: Elnathan. When did you start?

WINSTON: Here? October, last year.

EMMANUEL: Winston, Nelly was one of the originals. His record is still unbeaten. Nine fades in one hour.

WINSTON: Nine! You still cut?

ELNATHAN: Bust up hands. If I try, it will look like I used a chisel.

EMMANUEL & WINSTON: *(Laugh.)*

ELNATHAN: Any friend of Manna's is a friend of mine.

WINSTON: Manna?

ELNATHAN: That's his name.

WINSTON: Manna?!

ELNATHAN: They don't know?

WINSTON: What?

ELNATHAN: The reason we called him Manna?

EMMANUEL: If you dare/ tell him

ELNATHAN: When Manna started cutting, two hundred or so years ago

EMMANUEL: Nelly/

ELNATHAN: He had chronic dandruff! Tried everything to stop it, nothing worked! Just be falling on clients. Thing is, he was so smooth, no one complained! Pretended it wasn't happening, closed their eyes like they were praying with the white stuff falling, like Manna from the sky.

EMMANUEL: If you ever call me that, I will/ fire you

WINSTON: *(Laughs.)* Manna!

 // EMMANUEL throws a comb at WINSTON.

EMMANUEL: You never stop talking Elnathan. Anyway, how is Leeds?

ELNATHAN: Peaceful. Come visit. Bring Belinda.

EMMANUEL: Impossible! With the church and her community groups, even I don't see her.

WINSTON: Never met her too ya know Mr Elnathan.

ELNATHAN: Winston, she is so beautiful, it's not fair.

EMMANUEL: I'm lucky. What can I say?

ELNATHAN: : Speaking of luck, you guys could have done with some. Barcelona were useless today.

EMMANUEL: *(Laughs.)* Truthfully, we were rubbish. At least Suarez didn't bite anyone.

ELNATHAN: Even my daughter could have scored.

EMMANUEL: Now you are being disrespectful. Next season we will/ destroy all comers

ELNATHAN: What? Winston, Manna is making false prophecies. D'you have holy water? Need to cleanse him of demons!

WINSTON: Antiseptic spray?

ELNATHAN: Perfect.

EMMANUEL: If you near me with that bottle eh, I will show you/ what

// WINSTON runs to spray EMMANUEL, ELNATHAN is restraining him. SAMUEL enters and sees men playing.

SAMUEL: *(Laughing.)* What's going on?

// SAMUEL sees ELNATHAN.

Get out! I told you to stay away.

EMMANUEL: Nelly you should go.

ELNATHAN: It's a free country.

SAMUEL: This is my shop.

WINSTON: Samuel/ maybe you should

SAMUEL: Stay out of this Winston.

EMMANUEL: It's *My* shop. You hire a chair just like Winston.

SAMUEL: Leave or I'll/ throw you out

ELNATHAN: What?

(Beat.)

Samuel, this is the first time I'm seeing Manna since… since the trial… and Malachi would/ want us

SAMUEL: Don't say his name! Don't you dare *(Kisses teeth.)* if you speak… ah! After what you did/ he

ELNATHAN: Me? What did I / do?

EMMANUEL: Nelly, you should go.

ELNATHAN: I should go? Me? Why? After…

EMMANUEL: Please!

(Beat.)

ELNATHAN: Don't stay silent. You have to show him/ this is…

EMMANUEL: Please.

(Beat.)

ELNATHAN: Fine. Come and visit. Bring your wife. Winston…

WINSTON: Good to meet you.

ELNATHAN: Samuel I think/ there are

EMMANUEL: Nelly!

(Beat.)

ELNATHAN: Malachi sent me/ here to give

SAMUEL: I told you don't say his fucking name.

// SAMUEL lunges at ELNATHAN, WINSTON holds him back.

WINSTON: What wrong with you? Ya cyan't do this.

SAMUEL: Him! It was all him! My Dad went down for defending his own shop. That man was stealing from the safe, for six months! Dad caught him in the act, went blind

71

with rage, and at the trial, Emmanuel didn't say anything, didn't defend Dad, just stood there, silent, so he could have this shop all to himself. *(To EMMANUEL.)* How could you do that? He was like a brother to you.

EMMANUEL: Samuel let's/ calm down

SAMUEL: Three years cause of that Winston, cause of him. Now, he's come. This low-life, this pathetic excuse of man, this weakling, this thief has dragged his dirty smelly nyash into/ our shop

EMMANUEL: ENOUGH! ENOUGH! You will still respect your elders in this place! Here's the God's honest truth. Malachi, your father had money problems, huge gambling debts! Money had been disappearing, yes, but he told me it was Nelly and told Nelly it was me! He was manipulating both of us, told us to let it happen, that we could afford it, until Nelly walked in and actually saw him stealing. He got so embarrassed, he panicked and attacked him. Nelly had two broken ribs and a busted hand when the ambulance arrived. He hasn't been able to cut since. I had to scrape him off the floor. If I'd testified and told the truth in court, it would have been worse!

SAMUEL: Rubbish.

ELNATHAN: You weren't at any hearing.

SAMUEL: I was at school! How could I/ have seen

EMMANUEL: Exactly, you don't know!

ELNATHAN: Malachi asked me to come.

SAMUEL: Never.

ELNATHAN: You know what this is?

SAMUEL: What?

> *// ELNATHAN hands over a rolled up poster. SAMUEL unrolls it.*

SAMUEL: The poster. You used to hang them above your chairs.

ELNATHAN: This one is your father's, turn it over. That's his handwriting. Recognise it?

// SAMUEL reads.

SAMUEL: Think I'm an idiot? That I believe this?

ELNATHAN: It's what/ he gave me

SAMUEL: Shut up! Take this rubbish and get out!

(Beat.)

Go!

// SAMUEL tears the poster into pieces.

Get out!

EMMANUEL: Samuel.

SAMUEL: I can't…

// SAMUEL leaves.

SCENE 13

LAGOS // CHARACTERS:

TOKUNBO – Nigerian. Late 60s

OLAWALE – Nigerian. Mid 30s.

WALLACE – Nigerian. Early 20s

// 19:00. TOKUNBO is cutting OLAWALE's hair. 3 men eat in a corner.

OLAWALE: You know what's the biggest tribe in Naija?

TOKUNBO: What?

OLAWALE: Guess now.

TOKUNBO: Yoruba.

OLAWALE: No.

TOKUNBO: What now?

OLAWALE: Chelsea fans!

TOKUNBO: *(Laughs.)*

OLAWALE: Used to be ManU but the oga pata pata, Chief Alex Ferguson left. Now it's Chelsea and we have family across the world.

TOKUNBO: Extended upon extended family, and we destroyed Barcelona today!!

OLAWALE: Up Chelsea!

// TOKUNBO and OLAWALE dance and sing.

Them they loose oh! One by one.
Them they loose oh! One by one!

(Beat.)

TOKUNBO: That thing still anger me oh! Wake me up at 6am, and not pay for haircut!

OLAWALE: Don't worry about it.

TOKUNBO: It's disrespectful.

OLAWALE: I'll pay for that cut.

TOKUNBO: Thank you.

(Beat.)

How business Oga? Where you just come from?

OLAWALE: London, Accra, Kampala, Harare and Johannesburg.

TOKUNBO: All those places?

OLAWALE: and Kwame, my business partner just moved to London.

TOKUNBO: No wonder! You're looking rich.

OLAWALE: God is good.

TOKUNBO: All the time.

OLAWALE: All the time?

TOKUNBO: God is good!

(Beat.)

How person go wake old man like me from sleep, disappear without paying?

OLAWALE: Mr Tokunbo, forget am now, move on.

TOKUNBO: Move where?! This na the same shop.

OLAWALE: Okay. I get one joke, e go make you laugh.

TOKUNBO: Oya, I dey hear.

OLAWALE: One Hausaman, Yorubaman and Igboman are having drinks in a bar. Flies are buzzing all over the/ place. One fly

TOKUNBO: I know this joke already!

OLAWALE: *(Laughs.)* Who tell you? Did he invent it?

TOKUNBO: Person dey invent joke?

// Sound of a car horn outside. TOKUNBO shouts out the door.

TOKUNBO: Come back in ten minutes eh?

OLAWALE: What is it?

TOKUNBO: Taxi for my seven o'clock appointment. That one will become regular so this time next week, you no go find me.

OLAWALE: Why you doing this?

TOKUNBO: Scheduling?

OLAWALE: Yes.

TOKUNBO: It's the evolution of business.

OLAWALE: Time restrictions no work for Africa.

TOKUNBO: How we go organise now?

OLAWALE: Mek I tell you story?

TOKUNBO: I dey hear.

OLAWALE: One famous musician, name na Yo-Yo Ma, was travelling through Southern Africa. As he was travelling Yo-Yo Ma was collecting music wey cattle-herders dey sing/

TOKUNBO: Eh/

OLAWALE: Yo-Yo Ma hear one Goatman singing, tell the man sey make e stop, say he wan write down the music. He write small, then tell de Goatman make e sing again. Goatman sing completely different song! The notes change, melody different!

TOKUNBO: *(Laughs.)*

OLAWALE: Yo-Yo Ma say *Ah! That's not the song from before, why you change am?* Goatman say e no fit sing the same song. Say he cannot! Yo-Yo Ma ask why. He say the first time he sang, antelope was in the distance, cloud come cover the sun. Second time, cloud no dey there, antelope done disappear, so the song change.

TOKUNBO: Oh?/

OLAWALE: The thing be say, in olden days, before before, music was a live thing! E go *respond* to life, you no fit contain am! E no sweet for ear. Wetin happen be sey industrial revolution come come. People dey obsessed with time schedules, producing identical things, they started capturing music to put for boxes, to package time. But Africa, we no gree oh! That's the reason why we say we'll come at one o'clock, but no go reach till three. Time cannot contain us. The padlock does not work! It's not the African way. No be true?

TOKUNBO: *(Laughs.)* Na true.

OLAWALE: Ehen, so this scheduling, bad idea.

// WALLACE enters.

WALLACE: Good evening sir.

TOKUNBO: Get out of my sight!

OLAWALE: Mr Tokunbo?!

TOKUNBO: It's the boy that ran away this morning.

OLAWALE: And you are showing your face here?!

WALLACE: Mr Tokunbo, I offended you but na desperate times and I hope you find it in your heart to forgive me. I got the job. Here's double the price of the haircut, plus extra. Also I got you a present.

TOKUNBO: You got me present? WALLACE: Yes sir.

// WALLACE gives TOKUNBO the poster. He unrolls it and reads slowly.

TOKUNBO: *Zero miles per hour never looked so fast.*

(Beat.)

The poster from your Uncle in London?

WALLACE: Yes sir.

(Beat.)

// TOKUNBO shows it to OLAWALE, they make the sound of a speeding car.

WALLACE: Sir, I fit charge my phone?

TOKUNBO: Charge boy! Charge!

// TOKUNBO points to an adaptor.

TOKUNBO: Chief, you see it?

OLAWALE: Wetin?

TOKUNBO: Na de boys wey no get electricity for house, they come charge their phone, sit down, talk… five, six hours. They know people always come to barb so my generator will be on. Even for dark times, the barber shop na lighthouse, a beacon for the community where men come to be men mehn.

OLAWALE: *(Laughs.)* Where the men dey?

TOKUNBO: They go come soon, they go buy Guinness.

SCENE 14

LONDON // CHARACTERS:

SAMUEL – British & Nigerian & Pidgin. Early 20s.

EMMANUEL – Nigerian. Early 40s.

ETHAN – British. Late teens.

WINSTON – Caribbean. Early 30s.

ELNATHAN – Nigerian. Early 40s.

// 21:00. EMMANUEL has taped the poster back together, WINSTON sits in his chair and ELNATHAN sits in EMMANUEL'S chair. SAMUEL stands opposite EMMANUEL reading from the poster.

SAMUEL: *Dear Manna, I hear you are looking after Samuel. Gave him a job. It's more than I deserve from you. I'm sorry. I hope someday we can forget the past and look to the future. I hope business is well. Kowope. Your brother.*

(Beat.)

Kowope. Let the money be/ complete.

EMMANUEL: Complete

SAMUEL: Haven't heard that in years.

(Beat.)

This shop was the only place… everyone respected Dad… he loved it here.

EMMANUEL: I know.

SAMUEL: Why would he steal from his own barbers? From himself? Why wouldn't he ask you for help?

EMMANUEL: Men sometimes… I don't know. But that's the wrong question. The right question is *How do we move forward? What do we do next?*

(Beat.)

SAMUEL: So Dad was the one…

(Beat.)

EMMANUEL: Yes.

(Beat.)

WINSTON: So… it finish?

EMMANUEL: Huh?

WINSTON: All dis? De air clear now? Nuthing else a gwarn?

ELNATHAN: Huh?

WINSTON: Me blood pressure fe rise, me think it kill me, de tension between these two Mr Elnathan. So you telling me it done, it finish ere so?

EMMANUEL: I… think so. Hope so.

WINSTON: Good.

// WINSTON opens his cupboard for, shoves a bottle in Samuel's hands, retrieves four glasses.

SAMUEL: Is this Melissa's Rum from your birthday?

WINSTON: Special occasions only.

EMMANUEL: *(Pointing at the ground.)* For the Gods.

ELNATHAN: I can smell it from here.

// WINSTON pours till everyone holds a glass.

WINSTON: A toast, to how we move forward, and what comes next.

ALL: Cheers.

// ALL drink.

WINSTON: Right, see ya lyater.

EMMANUEL: Where're you going?

WINSTON: Pub! And you're not invited! Crazy Africans!

ALL: *(Laugh.)*

// WINSTON leaves.

ELNATHAN: I have a train to catch. Manna, please do come and visit, bring Belinda. Samuel...

SAMUEL: I owe you an apology.

ELNATHAN: Your father's apology was enough. Till next time eh?

// ELNATHAN leaves.

EMMANUEL: Elnathan...

(Beat.)

SAMUEL: Why didn't you tell me?

EMMANUEL: It wasn't my place to tell.

SAMUEL: I had a right to know.

EMMANUEL: There's a Nigerian saying: *Who no know, go know.* Now you know.

(Beat.)

SAMUEL: Well... I'm sorry.

(Beat.)

EMMANUEL: So you want to open another shop?

SAMUEL: Maybe.

(Beat.)

EMMANUEL: This was always yours Samuel. All this was for you.

(Beat.)

// ETHAN Enters.

ETHAN: Can I get a hair cut?

(Beat.)

SAMUEL: S... sorry, we are closed.

ETHAN: Just a shape up.

SAMUEL: It's past nine. Come back tomorrow.

ETHAN: Please I just… I'll pay anything, I need it… please.

EMMANUEL: Come on.

SAMUEL: I gotta go. It's my job to lock up so/ if you

EMMANUEL: I know. You, sit there.

// ETHAN sits, putting a script on the table by the mirror.

EMMANUEL: Keys?

// SAMUEL hands over the keys, shakes EMMANUEL's hands, and leaves.

EMMANUEL: Till tomorrow.

SAMUEL: Thank you. I'll see you tomorrow Uncle.

EMMANUEL: How was your day?

ETHAN: Fine fine.

(Beat.)

ETHAN: Er… How was your day?

EMMANUEL: My team lost the championship.

ETHAN: Ouch!

EMMANUEL: *(Laughs.)* I just pretend for the others.

(Beat.)

EMMANUEL: What's that?

ETHAN: A script.

EMMANUEL: You're an actor?

ETHAN: Audition tomorrow. Mum usually cuts me, but… working.

(Beat.)

EMMANUEL: Nervous? I don't look the part.

EMMANUEL: What's the part?

ETHAN: A black man.

(Beat.)

EMMANUEL: That's it?

ETHAN: A *strong* black man.

EMMANUEL: *(Laughs.)* You are overqualified.

ETHAN: *(Laughs.)*

(Beat.)

EMMANUEL: Why don't you think you'll get it?

ETHAN: I don't fit their idea of strong black masculinity.

EMMANUEL: What's your idea of it?

ETHAN: I don't know.

EMMANUEL: There's your problem.

ETHAN: Does anyone? Really?

(Beat.)

EMMANUEL: What do you mean?

ETHAN: Like I pluck my eyebrows, what's that got to do with masculinity? I see guys in the gym, pumping, tryna look like muscular black rappers, asking themselves *Am I a man yet?*

EMMANUEL: It comes down to personal definition.

ETHAN: They are asking *Am I a man?* not… *Who am I?*

EMMANUEL: Hmmm/

ETHAN: And then, *Am I a BLACK man? Am I a STRONG black man?* What's strong mean?

(Beat.)

I'm going nuts uncle.

EMMANUEL: Can't be that bad.

ETHAN: Worse! There are guys out there, lost, they look like fighters, but don't have the heart. Jay Z's got this line, You're *loud as a motor bike but wouldn't buss a grape in a fruit fight.*

EMMANUEL: *(Laughs.)* I grew up with boys like that in the village.

(Beat.)

What does your father think?

ETHAN: Never knew him. Left when I was six. I've searched online... nothing, but he's South African, think he's in Johannesburg.

EMMANUEL: Uncles?

ETHAN: None.

EMMANUEL: Who did you grow up with? Must've had someone to look up to?

ETHAN: Mum, she raised me.

EMMANUEL: So when you act roles, play black men, who d'you model them on?

ETHAN: I... don't really know. I just...

(Beat.)

EMMANUEL: *(Under his breath.)* Jesus.

ETHAN: Naaa... not him.

EMMANUEL: *(Laughs.)*

ETHAN: We can't be like any of those men; Mandela, Martin, Malcolm, Marcus... they are legends, titans, country-sized men. Compared to them we're islands.

EMMANUEL: Small islands.

(Beat.)

ETHAN: Uncle, if a man is an Island, is he still a man?

EMMANUEL: How old are you?

ETHAN: Eighteen.

EMMANUEL: Asking big questions tonight.

(Beat.)

You must have a young lady? Talk to her!

ETHAN: Don't want her to think I don't know who I am.

EMMANUEL: Friends?

ETHAN: *(Laughs.)* Tried. They said I was acting like a girl, told me to *Man Up*.

EMMANUEL: *(Laughs.)*

ETHAN: Are you married?

EMMANUEL: Belinda.

(Beat.)

She died.

(Beat.)

ETHAN: Sorry… didn't mean to…

EMMANUEL: Few months ago. I'm…

(Beat.)

ETHAN: Are you okay?

EMMANUEL: I'm here.

(Beat.)

Maybe we are not too different.

ETHAN: Yeah?

EMMANUEL: We who live outside our countries left because our leaders, our fathers failed us somehow, or the system was designed for us to fail. We're not in our motherlands… motherless too. Maybe we're all orphans here?

(Beat.)

Well, you're good to go.

ETHAN: Thank you.

(Beat.)

How much do I owe?

EMMANUEL: What?

ETHAN: Haircut?

EMMANUEL: Nothing. You owe nothing.

ETHAN: You sure?

EMMANUEL: Yes.

(Beat.)

ETHAN: Sorry, can I come tomorrow? Just to sit… listen… talk?

EMMANUEL: Of course. We open at nine.

ETHAN: Thanks.

// ETHAN turns towards the door.

EMMANUEL: Wait. D'you want to hear a joke?

ETHAN: *(Laughs.)* Yeah go on.

EMMANUEL: So an English, an Irishman and a Scotsman are having drinks in a bar…

END